The Heart of Healing

Bruce Davis, Ph.D.
and Genny Wright Davis

CELESTIALARTS
Berkeley, California

PRINTING HISTORY

The materials quoted from A COURSE IN MIRACLES, are used by permission of the copyright owner Foundation For Inner Peace © copyright 1975. The Course can be ordered directly from the Foundation, Box 635, Tiburon, CA 94920. Three volume hard cover set $40.00 postpaid or single volume soft cover for $25.00 postpaid.

Sincere gratitude to Doris, Paz, Alberto, Greg, Michael, Marsha, and Jennie for giving permission to share part of their story.

This book is possible due to the love and participation of Mickie Denig, Lonnie Barbach, Kathleen Vande Kieft, Elizabeth Rettig, Barbara Dunn, Mary Frandina, Don Travis, and Jana Janus. Our heart-filled thanks to each of you.

Bantam edition / August 1985

Cover Art by Kathleen Vande Kieft

Celestial Arts
P.O. Box 7327
Berkeley, CA 94707

Library of Congress Cataloging in Publication Data

Davis, Bruce, 1950–
   The heart of healing.

   Originally published: Fairfax, Calif. : Inner Light Books and Tapes, c1983.
   1. Spiritual healing. 2. Shamanism. I. Davis, Genny Wright.
II. Title.
BL65.M4D34 1985   291.4'02'2 [B]   85-6116
ISBN 0-89087-589-8

PRINTED IN THE UNITED STATES OF AMERICA.

1 2 3 4 5 — 91 90 89

THE HEART OF HEALING is dedicated to you whose greatest vision is for everyone to trust and shine in life as a burning flame. Living simply with your arms extended, your spirit is fulfilled only when ALL of each of us feels truly loved. Someday the world will stand so still as to listen to your light flicker, and then be surprised by hearing its own heart, beating in heavenly magnificence.

One day, an opening seminar for graduate school was to be the setting which a single experience changed everything that was going to follow in my life. A remarkable woman, who was a Shaman, a medicine woman for the Eskimo Indians, was at the seminar and was somehow—mysteriously—expecting me. Within hours I had become her apprentice and friend, beginning a relationship which was to last for four years, leading to meeting Genny, my spiritual partner. Together Genny and I journeyed, learning psychic healing in the Philippines and practicing daily lessons from an incredible set of books called *A Course in Miracles*, until our lives had surrendered to their own destinies.

Today, we know that the same spirit we experienced is opening in thousands and thousands of people's hearts around the world. Indeed, there is a spiritual revolution taking place.

Introduction

✦ ✦

I remember as a child sitting at my desk, lying awake in bed, thinking, "There must be something more." In junior high school I wrote serious essays and spent my afternoons riding my bicycle up and down alleys, looking into backyards. Everything seemed so tied up and desperate, with nowhere to go. My dreams, the future—nothing this world had to offer was enough.

Once in awhile a powerful feeling would surge through me, ready to explode inside. At these times, I had glimpses from somewhere of being truly special. But with adulthood, I never knew if these moments of incredible sense of purpose stemmed from arrogance, or were nothing less than God within me. How such a part of me would ever realize itself in this world was always a disappointing unknown.

No matter how much I tried I could never convince myself that one pursuit full of struggle would eventually lead to something better, that changes in politics, a new romantic relationship, or a fresh awareness of my feelings would lead my life to completion; I was never satisfied.

The choices in front of me never fulfilled the thirst that drove me forward. I was simply committed to the path of least compromise.

Then, one day, an opening seminar for graduate school was to be the setting in which a single experience changed everything that was going to follow in my life. A remarkable woman, who was a shaman, a medicine woman for the Eskimo Indians, was at the seminar and was somehow—mysteriously—expecting me. Within hours I had become her apprentice and friend, beginning a relationship which was to last for four years, leading me to meeting Genny, my spiritual partner. Together Genny and I journeyed, learning psychic healing in the Philippines and practicing daily lessons from an incredible set of books called *A Course in Miracles*, until our lives had surrendered to their own destinies, full of purpose and miracles.

Now, seven years after the events described in this book, even we admit that they seem to be of another world. We wonder how we can communicate to others that every experience described here is available within them as well. How do we fully convey that another reality always exists in our midst, no matter what circumstances our lives may be in?

We needed an Eskimo shaman and Philippine healers to pry our egos free of their hardened beliefs. Almost every day we meet someone who doesn't need such unusual teachers and experiences, one who naturally comes by his or her place and purpose. For them, humility leads them to the truth easily and quickly.

This book is for those of us who think we are greater than the flowers and the birds and those who naturally know an equality. This book is for all of us who are trying to control our destiny and manage our lives, instead of letting something special, our real purpose, bloom and grow.

Today, we know that the same spirit we experienced is opening in thousands and thousands of people's hearts around the world. Indeed, there is a spiritual revolution taking place. The climax of this age, we believe, is something far greater than the emergence of a single, great Divine Being. We imagine a world which sees that Divine Being in everyone, knowing that we are all related, closer than even family. This awareness of the world is unfolding already. Many, many people are realizing that each of us is whole only inasmuch as everyone recognizes their wholeness. Words cannot describe the unity and peace which is our potential and destiny. We know this revolution is occurring not through normal means of demonstrations and speeches, but by each of us risking to go into the darkest part of our lives with love and forgiveness, discovering our own beauty in the process. As the darkness is seen no longer as our enemy, but as having a unique service, surely the world will also recognize itself as wholly precious.

I

The Initiation

Chapter One

One spring, when the snow had completely melted, I began sitting for several hours every day underneath my tree. Each day the tree stood waiting for me. Although the park could be quite busy at times, I never found others occupying what was to be my place next to this particular oak in the park in Denver, Colorado.

Some time before, I had recognized that happiness is an internal affair. No amount of success or love from others would satisfy me unless my heart felt worthy enough to accept what good I found in the world. Each day it was here in the park where I could best measure my trust or fear of life. With the tree at my back, I had the perfect opportunity to practice planting my roots, letting my branches and leaves reach for the sky, while I surrendered to the seasons of my contrasting emotions and thoughts. It was here that I could receive the sun's rays as rays of God's love. And it was here where I could find sanctuary from the stress in my life. Next to this tree in a park, in the middle of a busy city, was just the right place for me to try to remember who I really am.

My mornings were spent working as a therapist. At one time, I saw personal therápy as a social movement. If people were having difficulties, the real problem was that they were not expressing their anger over their political/ social positions in life. I felt that when they allowed themselves to feel the natural rage within themselves, the liberation would revitalize their self-esteem and relationships. Then after reaching this point myself, I realized that there were many excuses to simply remain angry. Behind all of my anger about the limited choices I felt others and I have had was a lot of pain and an open area of unknown markings and depth.

So I entered a therapy process similar to primal therapy, to explore the repressed pain and uncharted territory I knew was within me. For almost a year I cried and screamed my feelings, as memories began to fill gaps inside. My emotions felt as if they were being peeled back into time, layer by translucent layer, like an onion. Towards the end of the process, I would curl up and grunt and shiver and feel squeezed, as if I were trying to be born or reborn. I continued to allow my feelings to be peeled back further and further, while I waited for the cure, which had been promised in the popular book of the time about primal therapy.

This continued until it occurred to me that I was limiting myself and the clients working with me. I was controlling our sessions by my expectations of what course to follow. I was, in fact, consistently choosing the path of feeling the pain of the child within, perhaps in some unreal hope of feeling it all, once and for all, and thus becoming free. The playful child, the intuitive knower, the creative doer, the one who knew all the other parts of the repressed being, also needed to be experienced.

My life and work changed. The center I was co-directing began inviting adults with an assortment of problems to come and rediscover their childhood. According to the age they felt, they were sent to different rooms to play with stuffed animals, cry, or draw—whatever they wished. Learning to recognize the age of their inner child and what that child really wanted was the crux of the process. Together we felt we were on the frontier of opening to a new experience, freed from our neurotic pasts.

I registered for a seminar at the Humanistic Psychology Institute, a graduate school which was later to be called the Saybrook Institute, in Northern California. I felt that developing my work through the process of writing a dissertation was the next step. The first evening of the week long seminar began with a film on psychic surgery in the Philippines. The patient in the film was there to narrate. He began by telling us that he had had a brain tumor which the doctors at UCLA could neither cure nor control. As a last resort, he had flown to the Philippines to see a primitive healer in the country. The healer went into an altered state of consciousness and working quickly, using only his hands, he opened the skin and skull, and removed obstructions from the brain. He then closed the opening, leaving no scar or any other sign of an operation. Here was the patient talking and joking about the tissue which was being removed in the film. People wanted to know if it were human tissue or, as often reported from these operations, only chicken guts. He laughed. "How would chicken guts get into my brain? I know something was removed from my head."

I was in a state of psychic trauma. A part of me actually believed and even understood the whole presentation. It simply felt true. My mind, however, was scrambling. It didn't seem to matter what the tissue really was. He was well! The brain tumor, which had been scientifically diagnosed, no longer existed. I accepted that as fact.

My politics of the time took comfort in the possibility that primitive people could outperform modern science in manipulating the basic elements of life. But I soon came to realize that the truth about the forces at work in the movie was something that transcended my inner intellectual dialogue. It was beyond my politics, and it was even beyond my feelings, no matter how correct they seemed at the moment.

The seminar was being held at a beautiful ranch

with acres of gardens, adobe huts, and two swimming pools. The participants included a Xerox executive who was leaving the corporate world, therapists of many types, a business tycoon, a Catholic Brother, and a woman, Doris. She immediately caught my interest when she was introduced as a Shaman.

Doris was the medicine woman for several Eskimo villages in Alaska. Besides using herbs, most of her healing abilities came from her psychic skills, which she learned as a child in Samoa. She told us that everything has a spirit: people, rocks, plants—everything. Her healing work included talking to the spirits around the patient. "Usually," she said, "the cause and the cure of any ailment could be found within only feet of each other."

As everyone was introducing themselves and telling why they were at the seminar, I listened to her story in particular. I had an incredible, yet disturbing, feeling that our gathering was for some purpose much greater than appearances suggested. We had only just met, yet we were instantly reacting to each other not as strangers but as colleagues reuniting after years of separation.

The extremes of human experience being expressed overwhelmed me. My head felt like it was desperately trying to hold onto whatever it could, to control my stomach. I retreated, as I usually did when I felt this way in a crowd of people. Finding refuge in my small cabin, I lay on the bed, curled up into a ball, crying, feeling lost in a wilderness of strange experiences. As I lay clutching the pillow, I suddenly felt what can only be described as a presence enter the room. It sat next to me, and held me. I felt its embrace as I would a living body. A sweet, peaceful feeling overcame me. I stopped crying and relaxed into—what? I did not know what it was. But at that moment, no explanation seemed necessary. In the calmness, I knew that someone was there with me.

On my way back to the main building, I decided that the experience must have come from a psychological need for a mother at the moment. As I walked into the room, Doris met me at the door, concern showing in her face. Looking deep into my eyes, she said, "Are you all right?" I nodded. "I would have come physically," she said, "but I didn't want to frighten you."

Instantly I accepted the impossible. I knew that the presence in the room with me had been Doris. It was Doris holding me, healing me. Doris smiled and led me into the room to a chair.

"It's time that we met. I've been waiting for you." She began, "We planned this meeting a long time ago, before we came down this time."

I nodded, knowing and yet not knowing, exactly what she was saying. She began to talk to me as if we had known each other a long time—or more accurately, many times. As I was about to ask a thousand questions, she said, "Sit with it. I will come to you this evening."

After dinner I was waiting for her, but because of group meetings and other discussions, we never had time to sit and talk. I went to bed disappointed. That night I dreamed I was sleeping in my bed at home. In the dream, I clearly saw myself in my own bed, dreaming about tomorrow at the clinic. Everything felt so familiar, so real and alive. Then I saw Doris appear next to me as I lay sleeping. I moved over, giving her room to sit down. She said, "I will come to you often like this, and we will discuss things in your dreams." At that instant I realized that I was dreaming, and the realization shook me awake, grasping to know where I was. I was alone.

The next day I arrived at the group meeting in time to hear more of Doris' story. She explained her work in the remote villages of Alaska. She said that there are no telephones, so when she is needed, she is often contacted telepathically. She is "told" the need and the degree of urgency for her coming. Telepathically, she transmits her own message to the village, telling them when and where she will arrive. She travels in her own plane, which she flies in all types of Alaskan weather.

Doris said, "I was home when I recently received a message that a little Eskimo girl had fallen through the ice into the water. The village elders were doing all they could to get her warm, but unless she received help within the next couple of hours, she would freeze to death. I knew it would take me at least two hours to fly to a small landing strip near the village. So I sent word telling them the time I could be there. Meanwhile, I began working on the girl as I was flying towards the village."

Somebody asked her what she meant by "working" on her? "Did you mean you were healing her at a distance?"

Doris said, "I had left my body in the plane and went to her and lay on top of her to warm her. When I arrived at the landing strip, the parents ran to me and told me that the girl was much warmer. But I knew only the top half of her body was warm, because I had not communicated to anybody to turn her over. I immediately ran into the village and turned her over and lay on top of her. Soon the little girl's body was warmed on both sides, and she regained consciousness. As I left, she was already on her feet and joining the other children."

When Doris had finished her story, the Xerox executive asked Doris about some unfamiliar words that kept coming into his mind. He repeated the words. Did she know what they meant? Doris stood and walked over to him and hugged him. The words were in a particular Eskimo dialect and were part of a message to Doris from her own Shaman, who was far away in a remote village. Doris explained that for him to be the receiver of the message had special significance.

That week of graduate school seemed to have nothing to do with academic requirements but was instead some predestined class required for me to go on with my life. The foundation of everything I had believed to be true had been shaken so quickly, questioned so expertly, that my normal self had no chance of survival. It was as if my mind were a building with a known number of rooms in it. Now I had been given the task of finding twice as many rooms. How many more rooms would I have to move into?

The conference ended. Before she left, Doris assured me that everything that had happened was supposed to have happened. She said, "The answers to all your questions are within your own self. You brought it all into the world with you. Sit quietly and practice being open to receive what really is."

I left feeling buoyed, and self-assured. I felt that I had been seen and acknowledged as at no other time in my life. I thought, "There really is more." I always knew it, but there was never anyone else there saying, "Yes. Yes, reach for it!"

Back home again, my clients all too easily occupied my attention, as they looked to me for answers, for the strength to risk feeling more. They wondered when they would be well.

The familiar pattern of my life resumed. My parents lived nearby, and we often had dinner together. After dinner I would stay for awhile and then would drive Josie, their cook, home. I always enjoyed our conversations, so it was easy for me to tell Josie what had happened in California. I asked her if she had heard of spirits and spiritual healing. She laughed, "Of course! You should come to our Gospel church. Some of our church sisters speak in tongues, and healings occur all the time through our great Lord Jesus." As I was telling her more of what had happened in California, she repeated over and over, "Jesus. Thank you, Jesus." Puzzled, I asked her, "Why are you saying that?"

She then told me that each month the entire church congregation puts names into a basket. At the beginning of the month, two of those names are drawn for everyone to pray for throughout the month. She had put my name into the basket, and it had been one of those picked this month. And everyone had been praying for me. So she wasn't surprised that "I had been touched." "In fact," she said, "someday you will be a healer and have your own church."

A healer? With my own church? Me? In the first place, I'm Jewish. And secondly, I don't even know what a healer is or does. I quickly dropped the conversation. Memories of the week on the ranch settled back into some infrequently used space in my mind.

The immediate issues before me were: to develop my graduate school program; to find peace in a relationship with a woman in my life who still sought other relationships; and to see if there were enough clients and enough interest to continue the therapy program. I had all the struggles, fears, doubts, and joys I needed each day—but I knew there was something more. I always had known there was more. Now this strange woman, Doris, had appeared in my life and awakened something which no amount of everyday mental traffic could deny.

Doris and I corresponded. That usually meant that I wrote letters which Doris answered by visiting me in my dreams. She did occasionally write neatly typed letters as well, as if to say, "All right, I'll do it this way if you won't listen any other way." The letters told me, "I am with you. Remember that I cannot come into your dreams unless you allow me to." What that meant, I didn't know. I had so many problems accepting a spiritual order to things. Every day rational thoughts and international news seemed to deny the idea of a divine order. Yet here was an unfamiliar aspect of life, in which a woman who was thousands of miles away appeared in my dreams and wrote letters explaining and knowing things about my day, things no one but I could know. Despite the chaos in the outer world, my inner feeling of being part of a harmony and order grew. Each day more synchronicity appeared: finding books, meeting people, and receiving letters with the exact answers to my questions.

Doris said, "Meditate! It's time for you to become aware of my presence, of something more than yourself, when you are awake as well as in your dreams. Night or day, it's all a dream. Meditate. Seek something greater! Your life won't just happen, you have to live it!"

The way things were with my current relationships, I knew I had had enough of trying to fit into someone else's pictures of what they wanted. I saw no reason to wait or compete for love. I was in love, but I had not yet met the special woman with whom I was to share this love. Everything in me was saying that if my meditation were clear enough, if I believed firmly enough and asked from that part of me that knows, the perfect woman to share this love with would appear. I also knew that I need not bother looking for her in bars or at parties.

So with the strength of the oak tree at my back, I sat every day for weeks, then months, feeling my love growing. I was convinced that the woman with whom I was to weave this life would walk right up to me any day, at any moment. This love was not limited to something shared between two people. I became aware that the love I was experiencing affected everything around me. Blackbirds in the park screeched and seemed to feel an urgency at the very moments some new dimension of love awakened and leaped inside of me. Even the wind and the squirrels seemed to know it. Everything in the park seemed to know it, except perhaps those people who walked their bodies through the park, while their minds walked somewhere else.

One afternoon I fell asleep under my oak tree and I dreamed that I was lying in the park. A woman with dark hair, bright hazel eyes, and a sweet softness came to me. As she lifted me up from the grass onto her lap, our faces met and we looked into each other's eyes. Then she said, "We will be together soon."

I woke up immediately. She was so real, so present. I couldn't believe I had been dreaming, but it didn't matter that it was only a dream. I knew! She was here! I had met her! She was in my life! It would only be time before we would be together physically.

Chapter Two

I stayed late in the park that day, expecting, waiting, and re-living the dream. Doris had taught me about the different types of dreams. There are the anxiety dreams which are created out of the excessive energy of each day, the energy for which I do not take responsibility and resolve during the hours I am awake. Dreams of intense emotion, she said, are a natural way for voices, which are caught deep within one's being, to surface and be heard. Repetitive dreams are like a record caught on one groove. The psyche is trapped in some inconclusion. Lucid dreams, where the senses create a world as sharp and intact as the one we experience when fully awake, are dreams in which spirit is communicating and integrating more of itself into this life and this body. Flying dreams, dreams which seem to break physical laws, were of the most significance to Doris. She said these dreams uncover our immortality and higher self.

The dark haired, hazel-eyed, soft and sweet woman had flown into my dream, picked me up, held me, and whispered, "We will be together soon." It had been more than a dream. It was all so real and distinct. So believable! I knew I would easily and immediately recognize her when we actually met. I already knew her, and I knew we would meet. I looked for her all over the park that day. The blackbirds were particularly noisy and excited. When the sun went down, every color of the sunset represented a part of myself. Each movement, each moment had personal meaning. This truly was a state of love. When I finally went home that night, I knew SHE was already in my life.

Days passed. Weeks went by. I looked for her constantly, and at the same time, I knew that time did not exist. Sometimes late in the day, I would begin to feel foolish—no, crazy—for making my dreams the center of my life. Watching television all night, sleeping throughout most of the next day, and eating just to have something in my mouth, could not silence the feeling. During these times, I knew my resistance was the strongest, but nothing could stop the quiet opening which was growing within me. I felt strangely isolated, knowing something to be real but unable to define it.

I had read that the art of manifestation required silent but firm belief. I must act as if it were already true. Surely, I had all the symptoms of love: hopelessness and periods of love's invincibility.

Meanwhile, my work at the clinic was coming to an end, and some relationships were ending. I no longer saw any reason to stay where I was living. Was my life mirroring my soul, a soul trapped in some nonreality? Or was I being told, being pushed, to move on to somewhere else?

When I felt Doris' presence with me, I asked her. I wrote her when I couldn't or didn't want to hear her answer. She offered no relief, no definitive answer. She gave me only the support to "go deeper within—you will know." I hated being told I would know. I was angry much of the time now. I hated that. I hated being so critical of others, so judgmental, so needy, so incomplete. After all the personal therapy I had been through, after the onion had been peeled and peeled again, there was no emotion or change in belief that could settle the dispute.

Intellectually, I thought it meant world views were battling for supremacy. Would I find comfort in the primitive world, or would I compromise and accept the relative security of the modern world. Doris said, "There is only one truth. You can spend your life resisting what you already know, or you can go deeper and learn more." I had opened the door to love within me without a special relationship. I had no choice but to go beyond appearances.

It was time to move. I was afraid that if I didn't leave the area and look for the signs, I would not meet her. I was also afraid that if I did leave the area impulsively, I would not meet her. With my belongings packed in my small Fiat convertible, I headed toward California. I knew by now that if I truly had chosen this relationship, as Doris said I had chosen every other major event in my life, even before I was born, then our meeting was inevitable. Somehow, graduate school and a new beginning now seemed appropriate for my growing affair of the heart. To invest my time thinking about when and how the physical relationship would happen was becoming less and less the question. It seemed to be more important for me to continue to ride this inner stream of consciousness.

Driving in an open car through the mountains, along the great Salt Lake, and through the desert alone, was an incredible meditational journey. I felt like a part of the changing scenery, open and vulnerable, yet as powerful and solid as the earth. I was to meet Michael, the Xerox executive from the seminar, and his wife, Marsha. Since the day Michael had heard the Eskimo words, he and his wife had also become Doris' apprentices. They were now selling Indian jewelry out of a mobile home, with a home base being a small cabin high in the Sierras. We met in Nevada and followed one another across the desert until we reached the mountains and their cabin. Doris had thrown a spiritual veil of protection over the three of us. We felt it. We compared notes, laughed, and huddled together before the unknown, which seemed to be circling our lives. Everything was changing rapidly around us, moving us into alignment with future events. Personal power gained momentum as we lived simply. The irony was that Doris would have us practice surrendering, letting go, and not knowing, as the way to final knowing. I was invited to make myself at home with Marsha and Michael in the Sierras. It wasn't long before I began a lifestyle of living in the mountains a few days a week and commuting to graduate school in San Francisco, where I stayed with other friends, the rest of the time. Meanwhile, Doris visited Michael, Marsha, and me in our dreams. On two brief occasions she flew into Reno to see us, giving us the stability to trust the unraveling.

Doris, Doris, Doris. More of her life was revealed to us as she led and taught us. She had been born in Samoa to a German father and Samoan mother. All the village adults were her parents. She was six when her real parents identified themselves for the first time. Until then, every nursing woman was her mother, and every man her father. The entire village was her family.

As a child, she would join the other children in playing psychic games. They entertained themselves during mealtimes by trying to lift off the tops of cooking pots without touching them. They would heal each other's scrapes and bruises with the softness of their own small hands holding the wound, as if all it needed was to be held and reminded it was all right.

When her parents identified themselves, it was because they thought that, in this changing world, Doris should have an education. Doris was to be sent to a private Catholic school in the northwestern United States. There, the nuns believed all children must sit at a desk, stand in lines, be quiet and orderly, and be silent unless spoken to. Doris became hysterical with the shock of such a cold culture trying to control her very nature.

She rebelled and bounced her voice off the walls. Doris had the ability to speak at a certain vibration, and her voice would be heard throughout the house. At nights she would creep into her teachers' dreams and repay them for their punishments. One day, as one of those punishments, she was locked into a broom closet. Doris took the head from a mop, fashioned a rag doll to represent the Mother Superior, and then broke its leg. The Mother Superior coincidentally had an accident at the same instant. The child's witchery had done its deed. The nuns had had enough. They gave Doris' parents a choice: either come and pick her up or have her committed to an institution.

Doris returned to the natural beauty of Samoa. The psychic damage, however, had shattered the inner peace she had known. Outwardly, panic was growing for everyone, as rumors grew that the Japanese were approaching the islands. Her parents didn't know whether to go south to Australia or north into Malaysia. They made their decision. It was Malaysia, a mistake that resulted in the brutal murder of both parents in front of Doris. The Japanese then interned Doris in a concentration camp in the Philippines. She was only twelve at the time, but she became an object of sexual abuse by the Japanese guards. The physical and psychic violence and the starvation reduced her, after a couple of years, to sixty pounds of nerves and anger.

Doris learned to channel the hatred. She began to practice her voodoo on the guards who mistreated her. Her fingers would become so hot they would leave burns, similar to those caused by a cigarette, on her intended victims.

During the war, she met an American who suffered through the Bataan Death March. He was a linguist and a man of unusual capacity for understanding and love. She was much younger than he, and under his protection Doris eventually recovered. An American west coast hospital served as a temporary shelter for her healing.

Through the telling of the story, Doris sometimes cried. She doesn't tell it often, but she insisted, "I know that I chose every bit of it. I am completing myself this time. I don't want to come back." Indeed, her life has been fuller than a hundred normal lives. And through it all, she talks about her faith, and the love she feels from the "other side." Her bony face and brilliant eyes reflect only the spiritual depths, and the physical scars are relegated to the past.

On a recent visit I asked her why it had been so hard for me to believe. After all, I had come from such a soft background, knowing only the best of this world. Doris said, "You have never had to believe. But more importantly, you have never been told the true beauty in believing. Remember, who you think you are now is only one moment, one grain of sand in the vastness of your spirit. You have known all that I have known in this life. Everyone has, but we choose not to remember. If we remembered, we all would live differently. We would all see that we are of the same blood, of the same God. Love would include understanding one another." I wanted to remember. I wanted to believe.

Doris had the gift of seeing clairvoyantly. When we visited people, she not only saw who they were in this life but also who they had been in other lives. Frequently, she would say upon leaving, "The reason you feel lots of respect for this person is that for several lifetimes he was your teacher and good friend." Or, "The reason you feel overly protective of this person is because, not too long ago, she was your daughter, but you were a woman, her mother.

"We are all family and friends, loving and hating each other through history. But don't think history is of the past. It is all happening simultaneously. We are literally repeating the same quarrels and jealousy, the same disputes as before. Only now we sometimes speak different languages and wear different clothes. Each new relationship is our opportunity to heal the past. In another dimension, the past is still occurring. 'Right now' includes the past, present, and future."

"But what about the other side?" I asked.

"I cannot tell you about that. I could, but it would be only words." Doris stated, "You must experience it firsthand. If your apprenticeship is successful, you will no longer be terrified of death. A healer is someone who has died and comes back to life to serve. An Eskimo Shaman must swim under the ice and come back. If it's a higher will, you too will swim under the ice, but in a form that is right for you. Pray for inner strength. Pray to be worthy of such a test."

Being with Doris, I could believe that she has died many times. That must be her source of faith. Faith and knowing are the same for her. It was so different from how I had imagined faith to be, something merely accepted. She knows. She is both King Solomon and a lonely shepherd. She is truly gifted and just as ordinary as the most ordinary person. Doris insisted upon being treated as anyone else. When people put her on a pedestal, she was insulted. "I am no different than they are. They have everything I have. Why should they treat me differently?" she would say.

"What about gurus," I asked, "people who have others worship them? They must also know that they are ordinary, and the people bowing to them are gurus as well."

"You've answered your own question," she said.

"I've always felt that true teachers would bow down to their students," I explained, "because they saw the same goodness in everyone."

I was going from one event or encounter to another. Writing, short visits, meditation, and dreams filled our relationship. Doris would write, "Are you aware that you are attending class at night? You have been at several of the dream classes that I have attended."

I wrote to tell Doris about a series of healing dreams in which spirit doctors and nurses were helping many people. Doris asked, "Do the spirits have weight to them? If they do, they are not a dream."

On another occasion, Doris came again into my sleep, telling me not to be so serious. "Enjoy yourself. Have a good time. You'll still grow and develop. Have fun!"

During one of my longer stays in San Francisco,

away from Michael and Marsha and the cabin, Doris flew in to be with me. She was on her way to a convention in San Diego. During her brief stay, Doris explained how one finds a teacher. "Everyone has three teachers available to them in each life," she began. "The first one is an invisible teacher for psychic and spiritual development. Such a teacher is with everyone. A second teacher in a physical form is given for similar psychic and spiritual development. The third is another physical teacher who appears in the life of those who are ready to learn to pursue out-of-body experiences and other realms of being."

Following an afternoon full of conversation, we took a walk. Out of nowhere, a group of children came dancing towards us. They circled us and disappeared as quickly as they appeared. Doris said, "That's an excellent sign. You are progressing nicely."

There came a period when I was distraught and impatient, a time when I sensed nothing and felt only self-pity. Doris wrote:

> *They shall not wither, my flowers,*
> *They shall not cease, my songs.*
> *I, the singer, lift them up.*
> *They are scattered, they spread about.*
> *Even though on earth my flowers*
> *May wither and yellow*
> *They will be carried there*
> *To the innermost house*
> *Of the bird with the golden feather.*

As I received her gift, I wished to someday be able to give to others the same love.

Several friends of mine wrote to Doris, asking her for help. Once she wrote back saying that when she picked up the letter, it vibrated. "In addition to the healing I am sending, try 500mg. of Vitamin E per day and three table-spoons of lecithin." Doris sees auras around each organ as well as around the whole person. For giving such diagnosis and prescriptions, she has often been censured by the medical and state authorities in Alaska.

Her spiritual counseling, however, could not be suppressed. She wrote, "I visited the records last night for you. The records are the spiritual source of one's negative and positive past lives. Plans and needs for this life are also kept there. These records become available when it is essential for growth in this life. They are found in a very deep, meditative place. I will tell you what I found the next time I see you." As usual, I was left with more information, but still fending for myself.

One day, as I was telling a faculty member from school about Doris and our apprenticeship, she told me about a set of three books called *A Course in Miracles.* These books had come through a research psychologist at Columbia Presbyterian Hospital during the late hours of the night. Finally, after years of being embarrassed by their contents, she gave them to somebody who had just recently begun to have them published. There were no general copies available, but I could read one copy which was on reserve in the Sonoma State College library. This faculty member showed me how I could check the books out, even if only for a few hours at a time. The *Course* included a workbook with spiritual exercises to practice every day. I could copy some of the exercises and then return again when I wanted the next lesson. In addition, there was a text, describing the source and philosophy of miracles, and a book called *A Teacher's Manual.*

The *Course* said:

> *"Of your ego you can do nothing to save yourself or others, but of your spirit you can do everything for the salvation of both."*[1] *"It takes great learning to understand that all things, events, encounters, and circumstances are helpful."*[2]

Every few days, and sometimes every day, I returned for more:

> *"Reality belongs only to spirit ... spirit is eternally free ... the mind that serves spirit is invulnerable."*[3]

The words seemed to satisfy a deep hunger. Sometimes I would sneak the book out of the library and lie on the college lawn. Then I would place the book on my chest, letting the sun and the words soak into me. The book's message was so simple:

> *"Abide in peace where God would have you be."*[4]
> *"When you have accepted your mission to extend peace, you will find peace, for by making it manifest, you will see it."*[5]

Soon I realized that the lessons had been incorporated into my everyday existence. Doris was now off in remote Alaska. She had had to leave Anchorage because the authorities wanted to put her in jail again for practicing medicine without a license. She reported having an affair with a master sergeant and having a great time in the snowy north. I didn't want to know this human side of Doris. I needed her to be perfect. It was too terrifying for me to know someone so gifted and equally human.

The *Course* had no such contradiction. The books gave my everyday life a new context, an order I seemed to so badly need:

> *"Do you really believe you can plan for your safety and joy better than He can?"*[6] *"You cannot but be in the right place at the right time."*[7] *"There is no time, no place, no state where God is absent. There is nothing to be feared."*[8] *"You will find Heaven. Everything you seek but this will fall away."*[9]

Something in me craved those words as others crave other satisfactions. The *Course* said:

"In you is all of Heaven. Every leaf that falls is given life in you. Each bird that ever sang will sing again in you. And every flower that ever bloomed has saved its perfume and its loveliness for you."[10]

Why were we never taught that life's perfect poetry lies within us? Why were we not taught, as the *Course* says:

W. -231

"What you see reflects your thinking. And your thinking but reflects your choice of what you want to see."[11] "The still infinity of endless peace surrounds you gently in its soft embrace, so strong and quiet, tranquil in the might of its Creator, nothing can intrude upon the sacred Son of God within."[12] T.57

My self-esteem had to be uncompromising to accept such beauty. Doris, simply by her soft smile and endless patience, and now the *Course*, reminded me that I deserved something greater.

One crisp morning Doris came again to California. We were sitting together quietly on the porch of Michael and Marsha's home in the Sierras, listening to the outdoors talking to itself and to us. Doris turned to me and said, "There's going to be an earthquake." No sooner had I accepted what she said than the porch and house began to shake. I had read about how different animals can sense when the earth is going to move. From Doris, I was literally shaken into an awareness that man could live in similar harmony.

That day we took a long walk in the woods. As Doris was pointing out all the different herbs and berries, I was noticing my mind being off someplace else. As she gracefully picked different roots and leaves, she smelled them, and told me how each could be used for different ailments. I felt overwhelmed by the sheer abundance of her knowledge. For me, education had always been something to accomplish and never really been considered my friend and guide. Doris was at home on her walks, and I was worried about becoming too tired, and getting back.

As we walked further, Doris picked up certain stones and plants and told me about "power." She had me hold different things and asked "Which one of these would you want to be in your possession if you were in a dangerous situation?" Then she proceeded to tell a story about how the herb in her hand had helped save someone's life one time when she was in the wilderness.

Doris often would give me different stones or articles from her travels in Alaska. I learned to carry them with me always. I would hold different objects in my hands at certain times, depending upon the feelings in the moment. Sometimes I would sit and meditate inside a circle of these objects and repeat a ritual Doris had suggested.

These times of feeling Doris' gifts protecting me helped me to spend less time struggling and challenging the elements about me. I would be less preoccupied with always wanting, seeking something more. Previously, if I were not anticipating finding the woman who came into my dream, I felt separate and empty. If I were not almost constantly experiencing or integrating some phenomena that confirmed my spiritual awakening, I felt naked. *A Course in Miracles* and Doris' lessons helped center me. In some way they were becoming parents of sorts, my spiritual parents. Infancy was so difficult, especially while I tried to maintain the appearance of my normal adult world. If I were not with my new parents, I found myself filling my days with other spiritual infants. As children we clung to each other to make everything okay.

With a special friend, Alberto, I studied, daydreamed, and played. Alberto had lived with shamans in Mexico and South America. He told me a story of an initiation ceremony in which a shaman used a knife to cut back a flap of skin between Alberto's eyes. "The more it bleeds," he was told, "the more you should pray to be able to see." The shaman continued to cut. Alberto could only see blood which was now coagulating around his eyes. He asked himself, "Should I pretend that I see something? How deep will he cut? I feel intense energy between my eyes—at my 'third eye.' How do I know to trust it? How do I know how much to trust the initiations we are all going through?"

Finally, he stopped questioning. The cutting, the bleeding, and the energy were accepted. Time ceased. Alberto saw a light approaching him, and at the same instant, it lifted him. He knew then that it could carry him through any circumstance.

Alberto and I discussed the process of surrender. We saw the balance and necessity of asking for what we really wanted. If we just surrendered, there was no risking, no affirmation that God was also within us. If we asked for what we wanted and didn't surrender, we might not receive the highest good but only satisfaction of the illusory needs of the moment.

Alberto and I had decided to spend the winter in Europe and travel to Israel in the spring. In jest, Alberto suggested we advertise in the Wall Street Journal as shamans for an international corporation. We decided instead to meditate, asking the best to come about for us.

Two days later, through a faculty member, we heard about a German doctor who was in town looking for two therapists to work in his country clinic in southern Germany. The work would entail helping addicts and schizophrenics. The coincidence was overwhelming. Doris came into my dream that night, reminding me to ask for everything I wanted. The next day the doctor and I met. As director of the clinic, he was excited about my experience in feeling therapy and my enthusiasm in general. We negotiated each other's needs. Remembering Doris' advice, I asked for everything I could think of. This included asking that Michael and Marsha also work with us. It was agreed. We would have housing, a car, four-day work weeks, and great salaries.

Two weeks before we were to leave for Germany, I went up to the Sierras to see Michael and Marsha. I walked into the house—and she was there, the woman with dark hair and soft, hazel eyes. I couldn't believe it! It was really her! She was exactly the woman who came to me that day in the park. As I looked at her, everything else in the room disappeared. She was so beautiful! I had forgotten the grace of her presence. And here she was, as real, as human, as I could ever have wished.

I stood there transfixed. I didn't know whether to take off my poncho, hug her, say hello, or what. Then something shot through me and I began to feel as normal as ever. I took off my poncho just as she was putting on her coat. We introduced ourselves, and she explained that she was expected in San Francisco for a date. "Tomorrow," she said, "I have to go back to work." Our conversation immediately became very casual, so easy. Instantly, we were like friends reuniting and parting. She got into her car, put her key into the ignition, and turned it. We were still talking. The engine would not start. She tried the key again, as we looked at each other through the windshield. Michael and Marsha were standing around the car with me. As we joked and kicked the hubcaps, I just stared into our lives, watching something incredible taking place. I was seeing that the physical world was not letting us part until something else happened. Her car had never acted this way before. I walked around, watching her as she watched me, while she was trying the key. The situation was so awkward, happening so quickly. Yet everything felt as part of a script, written long ago. The car finally started. She left the car running while she got out and hugged each of us "goodbye" again. When we hugged, there was an indescribable peace. There was nothing else to say. She got back into her car and left.

I walked out into the woods. In the silent forest, I could do nothing but cry, choking on the tears being wrenched from me. I felt all my doubts, all the weight of my own judgments. How many times had I made myself wrong, wrong for believing? After all of these months and now, of all times, two weeks before I was going to leave, I had found her. I had found her! No, we had found each other.

We were together no more than ten minutes. Yet I know we both were aware that something special was happening. I sank to my knees on the forest floor. The pain of my repressed hopes spilled out. With each wave of tears, I felt freer and freer. Of course, she was in my life. Why had I let my heart's dream become only a fantasy? Of course, she was here!

I walked back into the cabin. Michael and Marsha had wondered where I had been. They could see by looking at me that my eyes were filled with emotion. They couldn't tell if I were sad or had been truly awakened. Then they guessed. "It was Genny," they both said. "She was the woman in your dream." They laughed at each other. "Why didn't we think of it?" They had never imagined the two of us together, even though she was their best friend. "Genny," they explained, "is already in a steady relationship, and for eight years has been working as a flight attendant for an airline. We never thought . . ."

"It doesn't matter," I interrupted. "Now must have been the right time. It doesn't matter about her boyfriend or work either. I know everything is exactly as it should be."

We all hugged and cried. We could feel Doris in the room with us as if she were laughing, and saying, "Why are you three always so surprised by what spirit unfolds for you?"

Genny had come to say goodbye to her good friends. I had come to finalize our plans for traveling to Europe. How many times and in how many places had I actively looked for her? And we met in the least expected time and way. It was all so perfect! I wandered around the house not knowing what to do with myself. I was so incredibly excited and feeling shy; compulsively talking, yet feeling a peace I had never known. Who knew when or where our next meeting would be? And deep inside I knew everything was okay, just—somehow—right.

I read in *A Course in Miracles* that evening:

"There is no question but one you should ever ask of yourself; 'Do I want to know my Father's will for me?'"[13] T. -129

Chapter Three

✦

Genny and I met again briefly at the San Francisco airport the day I was leaving for Germany. She was reporting to work. An image came to my mind—this would be the only time I would ever see her in a flight attendant's uniform. We had just a few minutes together.

"As I was coming home from Michael and Marsha's house," Genny said, "I felt as if my life were slipping away from me. When I was crossing the Bay Bridge, I didn't even notice that my gas gauge was on empty. I stalled. But before I could get upset, these two nice men were behind my car, pushing me into a filling station. So no matter what is happening, I feel it is a good sign."

We talked about our trip, and I suggested that since Genny could travel cheaply, she should join us sometime in the winter for a ski vacation. I did not know how much of the story of the dream to share with her. What felt most important was to be with her for those brief minutes. The dream, and then our meeting, had given me the faith. I knew we would be together again when it was right. All that mattered now was her awareness that I knew that

something special, something incredible, was within her.
We said the most in our quiet moments, sitting together.
As we parted, I reached into my pocket and felt a small,
smooth stone with a carving in it. I did not know how it
got there, but it felt important to give it to her. I told her
to hold onto it until we met again. Genny looked at the
rock in disbelief. She hugged me as she said goodbye, and
I saw a beautiful calmness about her as I left for the
plane.

By the time the plane landed in New York, I had a
long letter all ready to put in the mail. With an ocean
soon between us, I felt safe enough to risk sharing the
dream. It was so real for me, that the briefness of our
relationship no longer inhibited me. A few weeks later I
received Genny's letter. In it she wrote, "I did not consciously remember or know you before our meeting. But I
have to admit that something within me began to shift
the day we met. I was crying when I ran out of gas on the
Bay Bridge. I didn't know why. I just felt everything
changing. Then when you gave me that rock! How did
you get it? You won't believe this, but as a child I had the
same exact, small stone with identical markings. Somehow it had been lost or disappeared. How did you get it? I
used to have it with me all the time. You have no idea
how I felt the day you left after you had given me that
stone. I met this incredible Indian man on my flight. I was
about to give him the stone. Then something said, 'No,
you must keep it for yourself.' I carry it with me all the
time. I sense that the routine of my work, traveling, and
relationships are changing, but I don't know how. I have
to admit, the frankness of your letter startled me a little
bit. But I assume everything is for the better. I will write
again. Because of airline benefits, I can fly to Europe with
a friend to go skiing this March. Will that be good for you
and Michael and Marsha? Bye for now . . ."

It was already the middle of January. I began my
new work with a full heart. The addicts' condition immediately felt full of feelings of powerlessness. They seemed
to feel so unworthy of having a painless life. There was

hostility, joy, and skepticism with our American warmth and inner freedom, as we encountered the German seriousness and limits of faith. We had been hired partly because we did not speak German, so our relationship with the patients had to be largely nonverbal. In many ways this made us more genuine with each other. We had little to hide behind, as the limits of our language abilities made us more honest and direct with one another.

The routine was that in the morning the patients went into soundproof rooms and cried, screamed, or expressed in any way appropriate the emptiness and early pain buried beneath their addictions. Our work in the afternoons was to build feelings of community, group solidarity, and to remind them that there was more than pain to their being.

It was only days before I discovered the trap of our presence. As the director was encouraging the patients to regress into the most extreme memories and feelings possible, we were there not really to build up their present lives but to act as comforters, so they could regress more the next day. The conflict of philosophies was too strong to idly participate in the whole process. The patients seemed to me to be naked and selfless, as if they were descending a spiral staircase into a pit of darkness. I had long ago discovered that the staircase downward never ends. The darkness is always present as long as we are looking for it. Indeed, to turn back and climb the staircase was the challenge that needed to be presented. It was much more of a risk, in my view, to climb upward to the angels and see that part of each other, than to remain in constant struggle in the dark pit of our raw emotions.

There had to be a balance. These patients were following the instructions of the director with the same promises of a "cure" which members of our center and I had listened to a few years before. We realized that it was not as simple as pouring out all of our pain to become well. There is a new self, a higher self, which actively needs support and development.

The therapy of opening one's heart does not relate

easily to techniques. One cannot cry and scream or express any other part of one's self with guaranteed results. Even meditation and other disciplines don't have unconditional promise. The needs of the heart are more subtle. The body, the self, needs so much love until we can breathe freely again. Love is caring for one's self and for one another. Then one begins to feel the love of the universe holding them, forgiving, and caring for them, as we do for each other.

Before leaving San Francisco, we were fortunate to buy one of the first paperback copies of *A Course in Miracles*. As usual, it counselled me exactly as to how to proceed:

> *"As forgiveness allows love to return to my awareness, I see a world of peace and safety and joy."*[14] W-85
> *"Nothing outside yourself can save you; nothing outside yourself can give you peace."*[15] W-118

As I remembered this awareness more and more, it became easier to see it in the patients at the clinic. No matter how suspect or how bizarre our spiral staircases seemed to each other, there had to be a bridge joining us. During groups we began expressing how we felt towards each other nonverbally. The touching, pushing, shoving and hugging began bringing us closer and closer together. In their climb downward, I began to see a purity in their nakedness, a beauty which I respected. As I began seeing this, coincidently several of the patients began reaching out to me. They invited me into their rooms and were excited to hear about my own therapy and stories of Doris. At least a few members of each group spoke some English, and they became the messengers of our inner secrets and thoughts.

Each day I asked for guidance to find new ways to reach the people in the group. Sometimes we would express ourselves in drawings or with games. At other times, we would create trust by leading each other around blindfolded. I would lead them into meditation, and together we would imagine a world without conflict. For them, it was only their imagination. But for me, it was giving our souls a time and place to express themselves.

The *Course* says:

> *"Teach only love for that is what you are. Gratitude to God becomes the way in which He is remembered, for love cannot be far behind a grateful heart and thankful mind."*[16] *M: 55*

The awkwardness of not knowing the language, the feelings of separateness caused by living in a foreign environment, and the demands of the clinic kept me in the present moment. Each day I had to come up with two or three hours of fun and loving exercises to lighten up the darkness which was discovered and expressed in the morning. Winter had piled several feet of snow outside, so even the sunshine and walks in nature weren't there to help me. Many times each day I gave thanks for everything I could think of. It seemed to work. Giving thanks kept me vitalized. Sometimes I would enter the room with the group with no idea of what we would do that session. I would begin by silently giving thanks. Within moments it would become apparent what all of us could do, without compromising their direction in therapy or my belief in reaching for our higher selves and attaining freedom, including freedom from pain. Creating trust within ourselves and between one another was usually central for each session. We did this through resolving conflicts with group members and conflicts about accepting the level of pain within us.

The director was certain that he was creating the new frontier of therapy. No longer were the professional and patient lost in the endless dialogue of analysis. No longer was the pain behind people's symptoms being ignored or dulled with medications. No longer did the past have to forever rule the present. But inside my gut, something felt wrong. Like many of the new therapies, the confrontation and the need to get into your feelings, which meant the need to be angry or feel pain, felt incomplete to me. The director was impressed that some of the patients who had been at the clinic the longest, almost two years, were now remembering their birth. A few were even having memories of painful incidents prior to birth, in a past life. The director had people investigating the information that the patients provided, trying to see if these lives had actually occurred. I was sure they probably had. But to what avail was this information? Where or when would it all stop? How much pain had to be felt before they felt love? Why not start right now, forgiving those with whom we are angry, whether in a supposed past life or the past of this life? Isn't forgiveness the final resolution that heals? These arguments were raging in my mind, as the clinic became a schoolground for me to resolve my own lessons in therapy and the teachings into which Doris was leading me.

The more I allowed myself to feel the intensity of each patient's hopes in some elusive cure, deep within me a voice wanted to rebel against what was happening. Part of me said I should say, "NO! It won't work!" Another voice within me said I should practice not judging what I see and hear. Another part of me said I must honor the truth as I know it, moment by moment, without being attached to being heard. Deep down, I felt the therapy had become another addiction. The patients had gone from the pain of being addicts into another personal hell. Granted, that this hell had some meaning and relationship to getting well. But as the therapy looked for all the buried ruins of the past, a beautiful garden in each patient went unseen. There was a flower wanting to bloom, wanting to reach for something new. And no one except the American therapists could see such a garden. No one, except us, was careful not to walk upon the tiny seeds which wanted to grow. I knew that no amount of recovered ruins, no amount of confrontation or pain, no matter how true it was, could force a flower to open. Only love, patience, and forgiveness would allow the flower inside the necessary safety to open. The clinic seemed to be ripping the petals apart, trying to get down to the truth. How could I tell them that the petals themselves, each feeling and each memory, were part of the truth. Each is something precious, worthy of holding gently, worthy of respect and love. I began to see that the healer has so much responsibility in both perceiving the problem and the cure.

At staff meetings, the director was often outraged about my lack of support of his program. He insisted I was afraid. "You must be afraid of your own pain," he said. "Otherwise you would not be discouraging the patients from going deeper and feeling what there is for them to feel."

In the midst of his heavy German thunder I tried to explain, "It's more of a risk to feel peaceful sometimes than to cry and be angry."

"Peaceful? Yuk!" he thundered back. "Let them feel peaceful when they are done feeling their pain!"

"How do you know if they will ever be done?" I interrupted. "How do you know if there is peace on the bottom if there is no bottom?" After hours of trying to reach some common ground, I admitted, "I know that we often cannot feel fully in the present because there is pain from the past in the way. But don't you understand? Why not try to feel the present anyway? Let any pain in the immediate way be acknowledged. Why avoid feeling good now, determined to look for monsters within us instead? If you're always looking for monsters, won't you always find them?"

Of course he returned the argument, "If you are always looking for this light you talk about, might you be blinded to the earth and the darkness about you?"

We got nowhere. I sought refuge in waiting for Genny, and in reading the *Course:*

> *"Peace of mind is clearly an internal matter. It must begin with your own thoughts and then extend outward. It is from your peace of mind that a peaceful perception of the world arises."*[17] W. - 51

As I was battling world views, Doris was still coming to me in my dreams. One night I dreamed I was back in the States, feeling very grateful for being home again. I was having dinner with my family. Doris entered the room and sat down at the table with us as if it were a totally normal occurrence for her to eat with us. We were all eating and talking, when, unexpectedly, I fell off my chair. I woke up to find myself on the floor, awake, but with my last thought from the dream still with me. "Why, Doris? Why did you push me out of my chair?"

Waking up in Germany on the floor of another house shattered my concepts of what is real. I couldn't figure out where I really was and which was a dream. As usual, Doris had successfully shaken my reality. Was she telling me not to hold onto what I think is real? Or was she simply playing games with me again, reminding me not to be so serious?

A few nights later I dreamed again. This time I was entering a cave to visit a peaceful, wise yogi. He was so removed from the world, yet so satisfied with life, so independent and free. I awakened from the dream feeling that the yogi was somehow part of me. The feeling stayed with me that day at work.

That day we were bringing in a new group. As an orientation, and a means of helping the members to feel separated from their usual lifestyle, which included drugs and alcohol, we were to take snow vehicles up to a retreat at the top of an Austrian mountain. Isolated on the mountain top, I felt as if I had again entered the cave with my yogi. The retreat also turned out to be a fresh change for the therapists, a break from the routine at the clinic. I was too busy to even think about Genny's arrival, which was now only days away.

After the first day on top of the snowy mountain, I again dreamed of the yogi. Just before I awakened, the yogi changed into a unicorn, menacing me with its horn. I was startled and frightened. Later in the morning I had some free time and decided to borrow a pair of skis. I was feeling too open to be with patients and just wanted to get away. Without bothering to check the bindings to see how they fit, I walked out onto the mountain and began to ski downward to the single chairlift. The snow was very deep, but crusty on the surface. At the moment I realized I had no choice but to finish the run, the tip of my ski caught on something, and suddenly I was tumbling. I felt something snap in my right knee. As I lay in the snow, I knew I must have done something serious. I knew that I had to rely on my own resources to get back to the lodge. After getting to my feet, I was determined to refuse to accept being stranded and incapable of getting back. I looked across the mountain to the lodge, steadied myself, and pushed off. I don't know what got me back within the reach of others and assistance, but I did.

I accepted the help I definitely needed to get to my room. I lay in bed feeling like a small, hurt child. I began to cry and a strange thing happened. As I allowed myself to release the tears, the pain was also released. In those moments, I knew that the accident was just another indication that the two worlds I had been battling with had come together in one confrontation. I asked myself, "How real is this injury? Does the spiritual or material world hold supremacy?" Before leaving the lodge that morning, I had read in the *Course:*

> *"Miracles are merely the translation of denial into trust."*[18] *T. - 203*

Almost of their own volition, the words kept repeating themselves in my mind. At last, I feel asleep. But as I left wakefulness, it seemed not to be sleep I was going into.

I felt myself leaving my body with its pain and flying back to the yogi's cave. But now the cave was somehow also a cloud and a garden. I knew I was in the cave/cloud/garden, but simultaneously I was aware of my body on the bed in my room at the lodge. I heard people in the room talking around me. But "I" was not there. I was with a little man, like my yogi, in the cave. He examined my knee. Then he took me inside my knee and showed me where it was damaged. I saw a twisted and torn muscle, and something underneath the muscle which was chipped. He began sending intense golden light into the knee. I could see the muscle tissue begin to change. Then the little man was taking me along a cord of pain into my stomach. "There," he pointed, "is the real cause of your accident." He had not actually spoken, but I understood his words to be: "Don't worry about your knee. It will be well when you are well again with your feelings." Then the little man left, and the next thing I knew, I was looking around the room. At the same time, I heard Michael and Marsha talking to me.

I opened my eyes to orient myself, before again falling into a dream, in which I was lying in a hospital bed. My grandmother, parents, and brothers were there next to me. I was unconscious, but I was asking them to pray for me. I felt hopelessly alone, separated from everyone, as I struggled with the unconsciousness. I knew I was dying. I fought to awaken. As something was pulling me further and further away from everyone, I pulled more and more. I fought and fought to awaken. At last I did. I was hysterical, "I don't want to die! I don't want to die!" I was hysterical, crying.

Michael was with me, holding me, urging me to go back into the dream. My whole body was shaking. Suddenly I became aware of a presence. I saw a spirit, glowing with a blue light, above me, welcoming me. I gradually let go of my fear and went into the blue light. I felt safe. I knew. For the first time I knew that death as an absolute end did not exist.

Again I awakened, but this time the physical world was different. It had lost its vise-like grip on me. My knee was slightly throbbing.

That evening, I read in the *Course:*

> *"If nothing but the truth exists, right-minded seeing cannot see anything but perfection."*[19] $T.34$

*   *   *

From that moment, I practiced seeing my leg as perfect, while giving thanks for the dreams, and for the vision—for that is what I knew it was—a vision. I felt protected and blessed. Many times before, weeks had passed when I couldn't even remember my dreams, and those I did remember made no sense. Today when I was coming apart, something else inside of me had created a balance, by taking me into another reality.

For the next two days, while we were still isolated on top of this mountain, I tried to retain that balance, as my self-control see-sawed from the painful knee to the gentle awakening occurring within me. The injury persisted. It seemed to be empowered by its own purpose of helping to make me stronger in my spiritual identity.

The retreat ended, and we came down from what seemed to be the top of the world. The snow vehicles took unusually long to get down the mountain because of the added depth in fresh snow. It was a long weekend ahead, and we were on vacation. Italy was only a day's drive away. We could be in Venice by nightfall.

Venice was a delight in winter. Tourists were gone, and we had the streets and canals almost all to ourselves. As we sipped chocolate in a morning cafe, we even enjoyed the rain and the pigeons. I realized how tired I was after the intensity of the last few days. But with the tiredness, there was also a strange willingness, an openness. I felt as if nothing stood between me and the universe. I shivered from the cold and my body's weakness. But my spirit soared in some new vastness, where I looked down upon myself and the world, and I saw that everything has its own perfect order.

I had a feeling that, perhaps, in that order I could find the meaning of my accident. I was certain it somehow related to Genny and her imminent arrival. Michael agreed to go with me to St. Mark's Cathedral to meditate, to see if we could find some answers, some guidance.

I sat down in the cathedral, feeling alone in the immensity of the church. The presence of God was very strong. I opened the *Course* again to read my morning lesson:

> *"You cannot understand how much your Father loves you, for there is no parallel in your experience of the world to help you understand it. There is nothing on earth with which it can compare, and nothing you have ever felt apart from Him resembles it even so faintly."*[20] T. -261

In spite of, or maybe because of, my accident and the dreams and realization afterwards, I felt so taken care of. I knew that the purpose of the injury was to slow me down, to give me the opportunity to reconnect with the true source of my life. I knew then that Genny's visit was not to bring love to me or create it with me, but only to bring me closer to the love already within me. I allowed the truth to move through me, and as I allowed it, I suddenly "saw" Genny's arrival and our time together in front of me on a movie screen. I saw us dressed for a wedding. I saw Doris and Greg (a friend who had learned healing in the Philippines) performing the ceremony. The ceremony was outside. The trees were glorious in their fall colors. I saw my grandmother and my family there. Love permeated it all.

Michael met me at the entrance of the cathedral. Before I had a chance to speak, he blurted out, "You'll never believe what came to me. You and Genny are going to be married. I saw Doris and Greg perform the wedding. We were all outdoors. I think it's going to take place in the fall."

Of course I laughed. As we compared details of our experiences I was surprised, but yet not surprised, that we both had seen such similar details. To myself, I said again, "Of course."

Marriage. To me it had always been an institution, something formal and unreal. Today it was no longer unreal. Today it was natural. Actual time spent with Genny had been only minutes. But I did not challenge the vision

Michael and I had shared. How could I so easily accept the idea of marriage to her based on that? But I did.

It was a long drive back through Switzerland, into Germany. It was glad Michael and Marsha were with me. And I was thankful for the gift of our friendship, a friendship that allowed us to trust each other to pray and meditate for each other. Michael had seen my vision. He had seen the same scenes, the exact details that I had seen. Because of that I could now move quietly through my fears and let my future—with Genny—reveal itself. As I sat in the back of the car, I felt that a child would also be with us someday.

Chapter Four

✦✦

The days seemed as only moments before I was on my way to Zurich airport to pick up Genny. My lesson in the *Course* that day said:

> *"Fear of the Will of God is one of the strangest beliefs the human mind has ever made."*[21] T_1 - /4𝒳

I felt apprehensive, at least until I saw her coming out of the gate into the customs area. I had forgotten the details of how she really looked.

Seeing her hazel eyes, her short dark hair contrasting with her white skin, suddenly she was real, not just the mystical image of my visions. She was here, divinely human. I watched her standing there, and for one irrational moment, I almost cried. She was too tall! What if, after all of this, she was taller than me? In that instant, I began rejecting everything, throwing it all away from me. She wouldn't like me. It just wouldn't work. I'm too short. She's too tall. This was ridiculous! My fears were totally out of control.

It seemed like forever before she finally cleared customs. Then I saw her high-heeled boots. A few inches of stacked leather had nearly done me in.

As we drove back to southern Germany, Genny sat as far away from me as she could get. Later she told me, "I sat there, holding onto the car door, trying to figure out this guy who had been writing me such embarrassingly frank letters."

I was working hard at being at ease. I wanted to trust that our time together would follow its own natural course. Knowing, or at least thinking I knew, what was to come, because of my visions, made it so much easier to let the relationship develop as it would.

I had to work the next day. Genny spent the day recovering from the long flight and the time change. Michael, Marsha, Genny, and I all went to Heidelberg for the weekend. There was no better place in the world to be in love. I found myself making mental notes as I observed Genny. I was surprised that I liked so many of the small things about her, her thoughts, her moods, the way she dressed. And I was surprised at how easily we enjoyed each other. Her everyday self was even greater than my dreams and visions. She said she had the same feelings, with one difference. She couldn't understand how I could walk with both feet off the ground.

Our days were mostly spent eating, talking, and just looking at each other. Everything else was only background. One morning we made an early start to hike around the old castle at the top of the hill. Centuries of intrigue permeated its walls. At one point, Genny pointed to some old doors next to a grassy knoll, "I wonder what's behind them," she said.

"I think it's probably where they keep the lawn mower," I answered. Laughter exploded from her. I didn't understand what was so funny.

"I was certain you were going to give some cryptic, mystical response," she explained. "I'm so glad to hear that you are indeed human. With all your stories about talking blackbirds and magic, I was beginning to wonder."

We both laughed and ran back to an old house where we were staying, falling and laughing as we ran down the long hill, rolling into each other's arms, in love.

We were swept away from our normal worlds. My difficulties at the clinic and Genny's awareness that her vacation was not endless were far away for now. Each day we climbed new heights, enjoying the love that we felt was being showered upon us.

Our days together were magical, filled with angel hunts. We went into back streets and antique stores looking for pictures of angels which seemed to reflect our feelings of heaven. Our lives were blending in a common dream of merging with the infinite, of being taken up in love's arms and being held forever. The world was only a playground for us to fly away from.

Small details, like being expected to be back at work the following Monday, were of little consequence to us. We had been apart so long, and we knew that we had the rest of our lives to be together. Genny found a couple of days for skiing with her friend, while I returned to the clinic. Each free hour we were off on picnics in the German countryside or enjoying dinners in small villages which were tucked away in fantasy-like valleys. Soon we had our favorites, yet we continued to explore for more. It was no accident that the sun was shining and the snow was quickly melting everywhere.

The clinic was located in a very small town of only four or five buildings, called Winterstetten. Only fifteen or twenty minutes away, another American therapist and I had found a farm house with a flat for rent. With a hundred cows and acres and acres of dandelions growing around us, Genny began to feel at home. We hiked, played and rolled in love. We weren't sure if we were in love with love, or truly in love with each other. It had been such a short time to know one another. But it didn't matter. From the beginning, we knew our relationship was about more than the two of us. We were brought together. Suddenly, the smallest details of life were beautiful. It felt like some invisible One was holding each of our hands, introducing us to the truth that love and life were the same.

I had told Genny about my apprenticeship with Doris. One morning at breakfast she announced, "I saw Doris last night. I was asleep when I felt someone at the foot of the bed. Then I felt my foot being picked up and pushed. I looked up and there was Doris." The woman she described matched her description exactly. I rummaged through my things to find a picture of Doris. Genny said, "That's her! She came last night!" It was just the sort of greeting I would expect from Doris.

Genny was fascinated, but Doris' presence was not entirely something new for her. Over coffee and rolls that morning, Genny opened up and proceeded to share a deep and delicate part of her past. "When I was little," she began, "I heard voices. I thought everybody did. Sometimes when I would hear them, I would ask my mother if she heard them as well. When she said that she didn't, I would sometimes feel frightened and all alone. But at other times, I felt as if the angels were talking to me, and it made me feel safe.

"My mother tells a story that when I was very young, I said to her one day, 'You know, you are not the first person to be my mother. I have been here before.' Evidently, my voice had such a degree of certainty that my mother said, 'That's probably true.' She was so giving to me, that through her support, my feelings weren't denied.

"A very special person in my childhood was my grandmother. She was a kind and loving soul. We would talk, and she would scratch my arms and back for hours. She lived in an apartment that my father had built for her over our garage. It was wonderful having a grandmother like her. I always had a place to go. She loved me exactly as I was and was always there for me. She taught me to be spiritual without preaching to me about religion. Her love for life shone so brightly through her that something very deep within me was embraced.

"My mother was often busy taking care of the house, our family, and also helping my father run his own business. We grew up in the suburbs of Los Angeles. My brother Tom had many different animals, including snakes, hawks, a bob-cat, and a wolf.

"In many respects, my childhood was probably normal. We lived at the beach every chance we could. We played and went to school. However, when I felt lonely, I would spend time with my brother's animals. Having heard things that weren't said, and seeing things that others didn't, I sometimes felt that only his animals could understand me. Deep within me, I felt my life had a divine purpose. Having had no one to explain it to brought me closer to God.

"I loved my father very much, even though I never really knew him. He was a welder and very busy working all of the time, or so it seemed. But the moments that I do remember are very dear to me. I was always amazed at how he could build and create things out of metal, including his own plane. At the beach, it was exciting to see him walk on his hands for a hundred feet from the sand into the ocean, until I saw just his feet disappearing under the surf.

"One day when I was eleven, my father came to my room to say goodbye. He was leaving on another one of many trips. It was his birthday, and he was flying his plane back to see his mother in Illinois. But for some reason, it wasn't just another trip. I wanted something from him. At the time, I found myself arguing for my allowance before he left. He didn't have any change with him. I wouldn't let him go. I was furious and refused to say goodbye. Something in me knew he wasn't coming back. But how could an eleven-year-old know that? Was I just being unreasonable? I was terribly upset! We waited for his return. When he was a day late, we called his mother. She confirmed that he had left. Days and weeks went by, even months, and nothing, not even a trace, was found. The government searched and so did many private planes. One day, a commercial airliner spotted a plane in the Mojave Desert, circled and then reported the ruins of a small plane. It was my father.

"The incident of my fighting with him before he left, stayed with me for years. I know now that I wasn't ready to let him go. On some level, I must have known that I wouldn't see him again. He was too important, and I was too young not to have him with me. I felt abandoned. I needed his love and he wasn't there. My mother became busier than ever, taking care of everything. I was alone.

"When I was fifteen, I met Bill. I opened up to him more than anyone else since my father's death. I dated others in high school but spent most of my time with him. My mother eventually remarried a man who had been her high school sweetheart many years before. Their marriage took place just before I graduated. Soon afterwards, we moved to Ohio. Bill came too. Although we were together, I wanted so much to go back to California. That fall I moved back. Soon afterwards, Bill was drafted, and then sent to Viet Nam. I went to college to get my degree in psychology. Then one day, I received word that Bill had been killed. Deep within me, the pain hit! I wondered, 'Does this mean that each person I truly love will be taken from me? Do I dare love again?'

"After going through the pain, I began to feel an inner strength. Life went on, and love came to me in so many ways. I was grateful!

"I joined the airlines and flew for many years. One day the pilot that was on our flight, knowing my last name, asked me if my father's plane was the one found in the Mojave Desert. He went on describing much more than I ever knew. I looked at him in amazement. 'How do you know all of that?' I asked.

" 'I was the one who found him,' he replied.

"It wasn't long after that incident that my grandmother died. All that I had felt as a child was confirmed for me when she passed away. At her funeral, I remember looking at her body, and crying. Suddenly, standing in front of me, as real as you are sitting there, she appeared. She said, 'Don't be sad for me. I am exactly where I want to be. I am happy.'

"I was shocked that no one else could see her. Her talking to me felt strangely natural, as if I had known all along that there was truly something more than what appeared to be—that death did not exist. Suddenly, the loss of my father, my boyfriend, and my grandmother felt different. I didn't really lose them. It's hard to say, but I felt I wasn't alone. The voices, and the angels I felt when I was a little girl, weren't imaginary. The angels really did hold me that night.

"My father's strength, Bill's love, my grandmother—they are still with me. The love, the qualities they opened in me, were mine and are with me always. But something was still missing. I always knew that there was something more for me, something important for me to do."

Our two weeks together had begun to confirm what was missing for Genny. The test now was to arrange our lives to have a chance to really be with one another. Genny made the decision to leave her life in California and come to live with me in Germany. She flew back to the States with quite a formidable list of things to do in the following two weeks. It would be painful and miraculous if she could accomplish it all easily. She had to tell her boyfriend about her new relationship. She had to get a leave from her job, rent her apartment, and store her car and belongings. I could tell it was difficult for her, that she felt she was having to give up everything, including her security and possessions. There was this excitement and glow from within her, which I was certain was giving us both the strength to go through what we had to complete.

Once home, she called her boyfriend, who by now was suspecting the worst. She hated being in the position she was in. Somehow it all had to be for the best. The pain of separation was with them both. But she knew in her heart it was over. In order to avoid his attempts of trying to get her to change her mind, she decided to take a few days vacation, with friends, in Mexico. There she could rest and contemplate a strategy to complete her affairs, in order to return to Europe.

One beautiful sun-filled day was spent at a deserted beach with her friends, far from anywhere. Genny's first thought was not to go into the ocean, but moments later she found herself running and diving right in. Soon afterwards, she felt a strong undertow pulling her under. She was waving frantically to her friends, who misinterpreted her gestures as an invitation to come and enjoy the water. She was pulled deeper and deeper into the ocean's grip. No longer able to fight the undertow, she knew she had to take a breath at that moment. She surrendered all of herself, even her life, to the sea. She took a breath. At that instant, out of nowhere, she found herself above the water, being pulled to the shore. In Genny's words, "I had no choice but to surrender to the sea. It was the final test. Was I willing to give up everything, even my life? I lay crying on the sand, knowing now, more than ever, that my life had just begun."

On her return home, she stopped in Dallas, where her mother was living at the time, to let her know of her decision. How could she explain that she was leaving her job, her apartment, and her friends to be with a man she had known for only two weeks? Genny prayed for strength, for the words to come through her. As she sat with her mother, she found herself saying things she had never heard before. The words had a truth so deep, that she knew all of this had to be from a higher will and that somehow her mother would be relieved of her fears. That night her mother had a very unusual dream. She dreamt that Genny's father was in the room with her. He said, very simply, "Don't worry about Genny. She's doing exactly what she should be doing." The next morning, upon confessing her dream, everyone felt that, indeed, something genuine was taking place.

In Germany, meanwhile, I felt as if I had been placed on hold as I waited for Genny's return. There wasn't time for letters, but I had to somehow let her know that what we felt was all true. My worst fear was that when she returned to the pressures of her life, she might decide to postpone or reject our romance. Of course, that was not the case. Though an ocean separated us, we were within inches of each other.

One day before going to call her, I sat on my bed and meditated. I wanted to visit her in her apartment and let her know I would be calling. As if hitting a switch inside of me, I saw her lying in bed in her apartment. She was wearing a pink nightgown. I told her I would be calling. Minutes later, I was ringing her. She picked up the receiver after one ring and said, "Hello Bruce!" We laughed at our intuitive connection. We had not planned on the phone call. I told her about the pink negligee. And she admitted she heard me saying that I was about to call.

The incident gave both of us renewed energy. Genny could now finish resolving loose ends, and I could trust that only the best was unfolding.

Our meeting at the Zurich airport two weeks later was so different. I rushed her off her feet, and we immediately headed for the closest inn, uniting all of our being once again.

Spring had changed everything, including the mood at the clinic. Genny quickly became friends with many of the patients. One special man named Andy, who spent most of his time with little green men, often accompanied us on walks to the river. There, the three of us played a game of throwing our craziness into the water and watching it go downstream. After the ritual, we all felt much better.

Weekends never came too soon, as we sped off to visit different Swiss lakes, basked in the sun under the snowcapped Alps, and sneaked into small, tucked-away churches, just to sit and meditate and enjoy the *Course*.

Michael, Marsha, and I had a two week vacation coming. We all knew this was our chance to go to Israel. We had visited Dachau, the concentration camp, a few weeks before. Man's potential for evil reminded us that, indeed, Heaven and Hell were on earth. What lower consciousness could we sink to? Knowing that all violence towards others is also violence to one's self, the atonement for the killing was beyond our imagination.

What shocked me the most was the town around the camp. Dachau, like many of the other camps, was not hidden far away and run by a few monsters, but was neatly planted in the midst of German society. Its walls were literally surrounded by gardens from neighboring family homes. That image haunted me for days. How could families lead normal lives only yards away from the mayhem? Then one night, while watching a newscast, I found myself watching a segment of starving children, while continuing to eat a delicious dinner. How easy it was for me to find excuses and ignore others' pain. Dachau was a village which was not that different from the global village we live in today. How deep within us does our insensitivity run? Who is really committed enough and giving enough to know for certain it would never happen again?

During those days, I was reading over and over again in the *Course* that we know God only through forgiveness.

In Israel, oddly enough, we felt many of the same feelings of Heaven and Hell on earth. Guns were everywhere. Every group of children had armed guards to protect them. These scenes felt peculiarly symbolic. The religious struggle of the Israelis seemed to be involved so much with land and rights, and so little with God and love. The Holy places, which all sides so desperately wanted, felt strangely empty of holiness. It was a sad irony. Here, where the greatest teachers of God's beauty and faith once lived, we saw a situation in which all sides found their only strength and security in their armies and their mutual hatred. All the contradictions of the world seemed to come to a point of crisis in the Holy Land. The Israelis and their enemies demonstrated for us the fears of the lower self and the teachings of the higher self in conflict. We could feel all sides to the dilemma. Nowhere did we meet either Jew or Arab and feel the heart of a living God, a God of forgiveness and caring, a God whose breath was within us all. The world's greatest religions had been born from a single seed right here. Centuries later, their followers were still fighting over parts of the garden, forgetting the seed from which they had all come.

My expectations had been too great. I had expected to have a great encounter with God's presence here in the birthplace of these great faiths. One day my lesson in the *Course* had words for everything I was experiencing:

> *"If you are trusting in your own strength, you have every reason to be apprehensive, anxious, and fearful."*[22] T.-75

A day later, after hours of traveling, I picked up the *Course*, and again it was talking specifically to me:

> *"You are not really capable of being tired, but you are very capable of wearying yourself. The strain of constant judgment is virtually intolerable."*[23] T.-43

It was true. My own judgments were keeping me separated from my higher self and from Israel.

It was a relief when we passed through security to board our plane for home. When we returned to our farm house in the German countryside, we left the remnants of sadness outside. Once again, Swiss lakes and out-of-the-way valleys captured our attention. We were in love, and it felt as if the whole world was cheering for us.

As I had supported Genny in taking a leave from her work, she was now helping me to see the obvious—it was time for me to consider doing the same. Neither of us knew what was next. While we waited to find out, we pooled our savings and bought a car from a neighboring farmer. We packed all of our belongings in the trunk, thinking we would travel for at least two months. First, we would go to San Marco Square, where I had the vision of our marriage. After that, we would travel wherever we felt inspired to go.

Each evening I would stop at a different hotel and begin to describe my fantasy of the day to the desk clerk.

For example, I would say, "I heard that there is a small inn right beside the lake that is very reasonable and not too far from town, but I have forgotten the name. Can you help me?" We were amazed at how magically the fantasies translated into reality.

We visited Venice, Florence, a small villa outside of Siena. The trip progressed as if it had all been precisely and lovingly prepared for us. Our fantasies were rewarded each time with something even greater. We were seemingly on the divine highway of our future.

Then one afternoon, somewhere in northern Italy, our car just stopped in the middle of the highway, without any warning. We waited on the side of the road for an angel, posing as a human, to pick us up. We waited for several hours, when finally a tow truck came by and took us to a garage. Thinking we were German, because of the license plates, the mechanic announced that the car was "kaput," without hope. We couldn't believe it! All of our savings gone, just like that? We unloaded all our belongings and took a train back to Germany. We tried to be proud of ourselves for believing we were still on God's highway, perhaps just a little detoured.

Doris was waiting for us back at the farmhouse. If losing the car was unexpected, Doris's arrival was even more out of context. Yet, it also seemed the most natural thing that could happen. She was almost off-handed as she greeted me, and then she turned to embrace Genny. They held each other as if they were best friends meeting once again. Doris hadn't even waited for an introduction. Her first words to Genny were, "Do you remember the night I visited you?"

We played and partied all night, and for awhile we forgot that we had left our car, which was all our savings, on the side of the road in Italy.

The next day Doris told us the story of what happened to her in San Francisco, while she was recuperating from the war.

The older man she had met in the prison camp stayed with her in San Francisco. He helped nurse her back to health and married her soon afterwards. Neither of them felt at home in the United States, but where should they go? Security to them meant finding a place where their spirits could be at home. They desperately needed an environment that responded to their sensitivity. Only in such a place could Doris regain her strength and the will to live.

In her meditations, she began having visions of the jungles of Ecuador. As she pursued the information that she was receiving, she learned that she was to go to the jungle she had seen in her vision, to live with the Jivaro Indians. They both knew that the Jivaros were headhunters. They also knew it was in their future. They had heard that a group of people from an oil company had recently made contact with the village and had then disappeared. But Doris' husband had a vision of walking on the jungle floors wearing their own heads. They took that as an invitation to proceed.

Their journey began with a flight to Quito, followed by a bus ride. They then traveled by canoe for days up rivers tucked away in the wilderness. Finally, they were on a raft, deep into Ecuador. They were constantly feeling as if many eyes were watching them. So they stripped off their clothes and threw their belongings overboard. They wanted the Indians to know that they were leaving their past behind. They spent several days poling their raft in this totally exposed condition, cautious, but going still deeper into the jungle. One day they came to a spot on the river where several well-defined paths led into the forest. They left the raft and climbed up the riverbed. Wild berries were everywhere, and they picked them and mashed them all over their bodies. They made offerings and prayers to the trees surrounding the spot, and then gathered roots and greens to eat. That night they slept buried in the sand of the riverbank, still feeling as if they were being observed.

They awoke to find that trenches, about half a foot deep, had been dug around their heads. They had heard or felt nothing in their sleep. At the bottom of the trenches they found herbs and berries. Was it a warning of some kind? They decided to accept the food as gifts. Now should they wait, or should they start into the jungle looking for the village?

They selected a path and began to walk miles into the jungle. Every so often they found a dead animal on the path in front of them. Were the animals a warning? Looking closely they saw darts, poisoned, they guessed, near each dead animal. Deciding the animals were a guide to pass safely, they bowed with each encounter and continued respectfully. At last they came to a deserted village.

It seemed deserted, but again they felt eyes observing from the bushes. Doris and her husband sat naked, back to back, and made low gutteral sounds, traditional worship sounds of different tribes Doris had known in the South Pacific. Doris began to make the sounds of animals. Soon children emerged from the jungle cover. Sitting quietly, Doris began to create the psychic image of a tent. In her mind, she pictured the flapping of the tent as a welcome. The children reacted—they could see it. Various animals were visualized, and the children began to call the names of the animals. Next she made alligator sounds, and the women, followed by the men, came out of the jungle. Doris and her husband continued to sit unmoving.

Men walked up to Doris' husband and began to touch him all over. Doris was led away to be examined by the women. It was then that they learned from sign language, and from Doris' husband's almost instinctual ability to understand foreign dialects, that the village's witch doctor had recently died, before being able to train an apprentice. Doris' presence was an answer to their prayers. Her abilities were instantly accepted, and for the next thirteen years, Doris was the witch doctor for the village.

My mind was pacing back and forth, frantic for more details. Doris sensed my frustration, smiled, and said, "We simply accepted their customs without judgment. When they did occasionally make stew out of their enemies, we accepted that too." We all laughed. Before I could say anything, Doris proceeded, "I gave birth to my three children in the jungle. They didn't know they were

different from the other Indian children until years later."
By now, I had given up my wish to steer the conversation,
and let Doris finish her story.

During their last year with the Jivaros, Doris began
having frequent dreams of living with Indians in small
villages in the snow. The dreams continued, revealing
specific details. Doris had never known snow, and so she
prayed, seeking to know the meaning of what was coming
to her. Soon she knew that she and her family were to go
to Alaska. They left the jungle and made the long journey
to Alaska, arriving by boat at the port she had often seen
in her visions. In her meditation she had alerted the local
shaman of her arrival, whoever he or she might be. Hundreds of natives were waiting for her when the boat docked.
Alaska has been her home ever since.

Genny and I sat there, absolutely stunned by her
tale. There was so much more we wanted to know but we
were already so overwhelmed by what we had just heard.
Doris' story had taken up most of the afternoon, as we let
our little farmhouse become the scene for Doris' adventures. We felt that we were actually there, as we began to
know the part of Doris which is an Indian medicine woman.
After hearing her story, our levels of trust were now in
quite a different perspective. We knew the answers we
sought were deep inside of us.

To start with, it was necessary to forgive the farmer
who sold us a seemingly bad car. Genny prayed with me
to try to reach that forgiveness. Afterwards we approached
him and told him about the car. We were dumbfounded
when he gave us our money back and sent one of his sons
into Italy to tow the car home. We gave extra thanks in
our daily thanksgiving ritual, which by now was becoming a regular part of our relationship.

Prayer, meditation, and the *Course* had become a
regular part of our relationship. We each sought our own
inner peace in our own time and way each day. But we
enjoyed sharing the experiences which were coming to us.
That day, after receiving what we felt we had lost, the
Course reflected back to us our mood of thanksgiving:

*   *   *

"You are altogether irreplaceable in the Mind of God. No one else can fill your part of it and while you leave your part of it empty, your eternal place waits for your return."[24] *"There is a place in you where there is perfect peace. There is a place in you where nothing is impossible. There is a place in you where the strength of God abides."*[25]

T.147

W. - 76

✦ ✦

Chapter Five

✦ ✦

Our time together in Europe was all so perfect. Sometimes Genny and I wondered if we had planned it all before we incarnated. Only by being away from home, which was filled with everyday concerns, could we have indulged in and enjoyed our love's extremes. Having had this time together, we were ready to return to California and begin our life.

Before leaving, we had one special afternoon with Doris in the German countryside next to our favorite stream. She took our hands and gave us a blessing. "The road will not always be easy," she said, "but you will become increasingly aware of a presence that is carrying you through the most difficult times. Together you should continue to practice identifying spirits that visit you. See if you both sense the same energy. I will come to see you in California and we will practice more together."

Holding Genny's small, sensitive hands, she said, "You will someday be able to turn a baby in its mother's womb. Your hands have the gift of being God's jewels. Let your hands be your guide and teacher."

We held each other without speaking, knowing something powerfully significant was happening. We sat for a long time listening to the stream and the sounds of the forest. It was our farewell to more than just our experiences here.

Doris' blessing and embrace stayed with us as we began resettling our lives. We stayed in Genny's old apartment for a few weeks until we could find one of our own. I had to finish the paperwork for graduate school. My dissertation was a book I had been periodically working on while I was in Germany, which I had planned to title, *The Magical Child Within You*. It was almost finished.

Genny was getting pressure from the airline to return to work. She was confused and in conflict. Looking to the future, the only thing we were certain about was that we were in love. The optimism we had felt in Europe was gone. Our families and friends were working, pursuing their normal lives. It was difficult to share the source of joy we were feeling. Everyone just assumed that we were in love and waited for us to settle down and resume some normalcy. To them this meant that both of us would go back to work and school and continue our old lives. But we had changed.

The *Course* said:

> *"Beware of the temptation to perceive yourself unfairly treated."*[26] *5.2&*

It was good advice, as I suddenly had to confront some new requirements before I could finish school. Genny continued to receive threatening letters from the airlines, demanding that she report to work or quit. We wondered how we were going to support ourselves. We felt so alone—attacked by the world from all sides. The *Course* continued to serve us as we sat with it each morning:

> *"Your holiness reverses all the laws of the world. It is beyond every restriction of time, space, distance, and limits of any kind."*[27] *T, 458*

*   *   *

The gentle reminder was needed as we reassured one another that we could create a life without compromise. If we gave in and returned to working in situations which didn't serve us, how could we teach others that there was something better? The *Course* said:

"All real pleasure comes from doing God's Will."[28]

T. -12

We took long walks along the water in Sausalito and in the beautiful hills of Marin County, asking to know the greatest will for us.

After weeks of our apparently doing nothing towards finding work, our friends teased, "You know the two of you are real cute hugging and kissing all the time, but you can't make a living from hugging and kissing."

After hearing the same exact line twice in the same day, we thought to ourselves, who says we can't? At that time, hugs and kisses were what we had most of to give to the world. That weekend we sat down and wrote a draft of a book called *Hugs & Kisses*, describing the many differents ways to hug and kiss. Genny tried illustrating the text letting her hands guide themselves. Her drawings were perfect! Friends read the manuscript. Again we heard comments like, "It's cute, but . . ." We also heard, "Getting it published will be almost impossible."

An editor friend mentioned a publisher we might try. We visited several bookstores and noticed that the books published by that company were always on the front counter. That was where we pictured our book. So we blessed it and asked that *Hugs & Kisses* be accepted. We asked that it be a demonstration of faith and a source of income. We wanted to help others without being dependent upon them for our livelihood. We didn't want to be like other therapists I had encountered, who unconsciously resisted letting go of their patients and seeing them healed because of their own financial needs.

The day we submitted our manuscript, we had a picnic on top of Mount Tamalpais, looking out over the bay. We imagined our hugs and kisses someday being shared with thousands. The *Course* said:

> *"There is no problem in any situation that faith will not solve. Is it not possible that all your problems have been solved, but you have removed yourself from the solution?"*[29] T, -342

Two weeks later we called the publisher. He had briefly looked at the book and didn't think he wanted it. But he had passed it along to one of his editors. We hung up disappointed, yet something in us said, "Don't give up. Everything is right."

Every day we took walks and asked for the doors of opportunity to open. Our companionship held the part of each of us that was on the edge reaching out and trusting. We didn't want to panic and act from our fear. Sometimes, however, I would freeze anyway. I wouldn't want to spend even an extra dollar at the market, fearful of not knowing where the next one would be coming from. The freedom of my spirit and our needs for living in this world felt so separate.

We found a beautiful little white cottage for rent in the hills of Bolinas, over the mountains and up the coast from San Francisco. Our dreams once again soared as we asked for the best to happen. When we inquired about it, we found out that it was not certain when, or if, the house would be vacant. Our time for finding a new home was running out. We understood God did his greatest works in the final hour. But thinking it and truly knowing it were not yet the same. Every part of our lives seemed so much in doubt. We held hands and lived in the moment with the *Course* as our best friend:

> *"Heaven is here. There is nowhere else. Heaven is now. There is no other time."*[30] M, -58

Would we fall into the trap of believing in the appearances of our lives and live in fear, or would we realize that we were already whole and that it would be only time before our lives would straighten out and reflect what we knew inside? For weeks Genny had been having a pain in her abdomen. Intellectually we both understood that everything was okay, that her body was just adjusting to her emotions. Our doubting selves questioned everything. Spiritually we had to let go and embody what all the teachers and books talked about—letting our faith supply our every need.

My graduate committee was finding more and more work for me to do and more sacrifices to make before I could graduate. The airlines had no trust or sympathy for Genny and her physical problems. We found ourselves coming closer together as a team, battling the elements. The battle itself was having its toll.

The *Course* said:

> "... exempt no one from your love, or you will be hiding a dark place in your mind where the Holy Spirit is not welcome. And thus you will exempt yourself from His healing power, for by not offering total love, you will not be healed completely."[31] 7.221

Each day we worked on sending love in our meditations to those most difficult to love. We called the publisher again. Even though the publisher didn't want it, perhaps the editor who was reading it would. She said, "Give me time. I think it'll work out." So many blessings appeared on the horizon. But was our faith strong enough?

The next day we called again about the cottage and finally reached the owner. "Was it available?" we asked.

"No," he replied decisively. "I want to save the place for my mother."

Our hearts sank once again. We had only until the end of the week to find a new place. That evening Doris called. "I have an appointment in Los Angeles this weekend," she said. "I thought I might come to California early and visit with you."

How did she know how perfect her timing was? We

needed her guidance, and just her presence reminded us so much of the truth.

Sitting with Doris again, I became aware of how I had been trying to use my spiritual self to make my material world comfortable. I had forgotten to embrace the spirit for its own sake. Doris asked us to tell her where in the room we could feel another entity visiting us. Both Genny and I felt it in one corner. It was as if in our mind's eye we first felt something in the room, and then when we allowed that feeling to have a picture, we could "see" who was with us. Doris said to us, "Allow yourselves to see more details. Who is in the room with us?"

"I feel a mother, daughter, and an old man standing over there," Genny answered.

"The daughter is standing between the mother and the old man," I added. "And it feels like they know you from Alaska."

Doris agreed, "You've done well. They are clients of mine." She continued to explain, "Parts of all our relationships sometimes remain with us to learn more or to simply hang onto our company. Their spirits are free to travel, not only after their death, but when they are sleeping, even when daydreaming. This family and I were in the middle of some intense work together and they have decided to come along with me on my journey. Can you hear what they are saying?"

We tried listening. But our minds got in the way. The situation was too foreign for us to let go and listen.

"They are visiting us," she explained, "in an out-of-body experience while they are sleeping at home, in a town not too far from where I live. They simply wanted to meet you and be close to other students of mine."

It was good to be with Doris. We knew she couldn't solve our problems, but being with her left us with the special feeling that we were being taken care of. It was easier to accept everything as being in perfect order.

The next morning the three of us were making breakfast. Abruptly, in the middle of the kitchen, about three feet above the floor, appeared a small, black box. It just floated there. Genny and I were dumbfounded. The black box was as real as we were. We could only stand there mesmerized, staring. Doris broke the moment by laughing. "Why don't you reach inside it?" she asked.

By this time the box had floated a few inches higher, and then disappeared. "You have been asking for a gift, haven't you?" Doris asked.

I knew that simply the appearance of the box itself, not anything that might be inside it, was the gift we had been seeking.

That day we started looking again for a place to rent. Thinking that Doris' visit and the box might be our lucky omens, we really felt like it was going to be our day. There was one listing in the paper for a house in Sausalito. It was on a street we had never heard of before. We located it on a map and were there within minutes. The house, the only building on the entire street, was tucked quietly into a peaceful corner. As soon as we entered the house, Genny and I both knew that it was our house.

Doris wandered around the living room while we talked to the owner. The landlady was handing out pieces of paper for the other house hunters. We were asked to leave our names if we were interested. "You know," she said, "there is a whole list of people who've said they want this place. I tell them to sign their names and think about it, and then call tomorrow."

"We don't have to," I said. "We know it's just right."

I started to tell her a little about ourselves, but she interrupted me, "I've never done this before. I'm never this spontaneous, but you two just feel right. It's yours!"

There was even time for a celebration before we took Doris to the plane. Doris said, "I had a feeling that this visit was going to be quite fun!"

The day we moved in, we asked our friend Greg to join us in blessing our new home. We had been meeting with Greg several times a week. Greg told us his stories about his healing work and his experiences in the Philippines, and we all shared our dreams of the previous night.

Greg is a very large man. One of his hands is almost

as big as both of my hands put together. His sense of humor matches his size. He was always particularly interesting to talk to about the source of his healing abilities, because his upbringing and middle-class background were similar to ours. From the time he was a teenager, he had suffered from migraine headaches. He came to accept that life simply included this pain. He said that he used to be very angry so much of the time. When he played rugby at college, he nearly killed someone because of his anger. It was hard to imagine Greg being angry. He was so humble and gentle now. The Art Department at Dartmouth was where he sought his own creativity but after graduation he wasn't sure what he wanted to do.

That summer his mother had planned to travel to the Philippines to see healers. He thought it would be a great opportunity to work on his photography. He didn't believe in primitive healing, but he thought he should go with her to be of support.

He wasn't at all prepared for what happened there. The healers first worked on his mother, and then on him. His migraine headaches went away and did not come back. For the first time, he knew what it was to be free from the pain for more than a few days.

Greg learned how persistent symptoms are often helped with other forms of healing when Western medicine can do little. The healer asked Greg to stay in the village for awhile so that he could train him. Together they made many trips into the mountains to remote villages. Soon Greg began having unusual experiences of feeling energy while he was standing next to the healing. After being told about meditation by the healers, Greg began to feel unusually still and sensitive when he quieted his mind and felt his spirit within him. The healer explained that the headaches and his anger were just his resistance. What Greg called energy was a healing energy seeking to be channeled through him. The healer said, "You must learn to accept it."

We discussed how chronic symptoms, like headaches, can be a mask for deeper psychic or spiritual abilities. They can unfold when that energy is released and given somewhere to go. Greg, Genny, and I knew people who, after working with their chronic illnesses, began developing unusual psychic and spiritual gifts. The persistent pain is like a flag of some sort, calling for attention. And once noticed and listened to, that energy can be experienced as a source of inspiration, instead of pain.

Greg had recently returned to Marin County in northern California. He set up a room in his basement for healing. After two years in the Philippines, he had gained the skills and confidence to bring much of the knowledge and healing skills back to the States with him.

One morning when Greg came to visit, Genny had stomach pains. Greg asked her to lie down, and he placed his hands on her stomach. Moments later, Genny remarked that she had felt warmth. He asked her to close her eyes and tell him what she "saw" under his hand. She said, "There's an ugly looking monster."

"Try to go over to it and touch it," Greg instructed her.

"It's difficult," Genny cried. "He's so horrible!" Greg sat with her, telling her to take her time. Genny began feeling stronger. "I'm touching him," she said, "and he's getting smaller."

"Good!" said Greg.

The healing was about over. Genny breathed deeply. The monster had now turned into something so delicate and small. She stood up feeling much better.

One morning, a few weeks later, Greg turned to Genny and asked if she wanted to come with him while he worked. Genny went, assuming she was just going to watch. When his patient came in, Greg called Genny up to the table and asked her "What do you see going on with him? Where is he blocked?"

Genny didn't know. Greg persisted. She felt she had to know. She had never been in such a spot. She said the first thing that came into her mind: "He's blocked in his chest and stomach."

"OK," Greg said, "put your hands on him." Then he left the room.

Genny was embarrassed. She didn't want to look as if she didn't know what she was doing, so she put her hands on his stomach and asked him to breathe. She meditated, surrendered, and asked God to help her. Her hands became warm. She could feel heat passing through her hands and going into his body. She saw a vision of a tall, thin man with dark hair and a beard. What did it mean? Should she risk asking the man on the table? The vision persisted. As she said what she saw, the man began to cry and said, "It is my father. For years I have been running from him, from the pain of having lost him." He continued crying, saying, "I miss him so much. I feel so incomplete with him gone."

"Feel him with you now," Genny said.

Suddenly the man's stomach gurgled and he began to relax. Into Genny's thoughts came an image of this man being filled with light. It had happened so quickly, as if it had been a dream.

Later, alone with Genny, Greg explained that he had been observing her and knew she was ready to begin using her hands. That day her apprenticeship began. Greg provided her the space and clients to work with. It was up to Genny to find the commitment and spirit within her.

Several days a week she joined Greg in his basement healing center. Sometimes they would see six or seven people, one right after another. The clients had all kinds of physical and emotional difficulties. One day they were with a woman who had cancer. Greg asked Genny, "What colors do you see?" Later that day Genny asked Greg if he saw the same colors she had seen. Greg said, "I don't usually see colors. But you must acknowledge what you see." Sometimes Genny would see things. At other times, she would hear words as if they were appearing in her mind. She often would taste, and even smell, some truth about the people with whom she worked.

After working all day, Genny often came home exhausted and angry. She was feeling the stress of constantly taking the risk to express what she felt and knew as she worked with people. She didn't know if she was really helping. At the end of the day everybody's energy felt so confusing. She and Greg would work all day and never once compare mental notes and conclusions. They never took the time to relax and sort out all the energy they had experienced. Genny had adjusted easily to using her hands. It seemed that they had been waiting to be appreciated. But at the same time it was all so new. Where was all this leading her? She had been giving all her time and energy to working with Greg. She knew she had to give some concern to finding a way to support herself. She was also concerned that people would start to think of her as different or weird.

As I watched Genny going into this new phase of her life, I saw her softening, opening to something so peaceful and gentle. The angels that she could feel as a child were now again with her. Sometimes at night I could not sleep if I lay close to her. Her body would become so very hot. I remember that my friend Alberto had told me that it is an honor to sleep in the same bed with a healer. I began to feel what he meant. At night, especially, we would feel the energy in our bedroom, nurturing us. We both had incredible dreams.

Genny wanted her work to be exact and perfect. I saw her judging herself, making the process so much harder. Each time she analyzed, trying to make sense of what she was doing, the energy stopped, and she would feel stuck. She threw things around the house and screamed. She was opening to more and more energy. But just how was she going to be asked to let go and surrender more? Greg gave her almost no feedback on her work. He would only say, "You will know."

Genny was quickly using up the benefits from her job with the airlines. After so many years of a regular pay check, it was very difficult for her to think about going into a future with no guarantees. It was easy for Genny to see God working for and through others, but would the same be provided for her?

More and more during her work she began feeling a Divine presence. I was amazed at how naturally she would sit with someone very ill and not see their illness, but a part of them which was very special, a part of them which was sensitive, warm, and Divine. She would place her small hands on them and feel God loving them through her. Genny naturally found such a capacity of love.

Our relationship was changing. We found ourselves reaching for higher parts of ourselves, and less for each other. Our relationship was becoming a partnership. Our romance was more and more with the unknown, which was coming alive within us.

This growing affair of the heart was not without its doubt and insecurity. Like any new relationship, Genny did not know if she could fully trust it. Sometimes, she would be feeling totally peaceful, and then, just minutes later, the smallest disturbance would completely upset her. One moment she would be seeing angels and a few minutes later, when something made her doubt her abilities, her angels turned to demons. They were monsters closing in on her. She was certain that she was going crazy at those times. We held each other tightly. She understood that the monsters were only her fear, but they were no less real or intense.

As Genny opened more and more to her capacity to love people with all kinds of problems, she also opened to all kinds of barriers within her. If she were to help someone forgive and love their cancer, she knew that she had to love the part of herself that felt cancerous or out of control. If she were to help someone let go of the burdens he was carrying in order for him to breathe more easily, she had to let go of her own burdens as well. Each patient became a teacher for her. She realized that she could only see as much healing in them as she could accept within herself. As she supported others to become friends with the monsters in their lives, she had to make similar commitments.

All the stereotypes of a healer seemed so wrong. When we thought of a healer, the image that usually came

to mind was one of the charismatic evangelists on television with people throwing away their crutches and wheel-
chairs, running and dancing up the aisles. No wonder
Genny felt shaky about the ultimate result of all her work.

But at the opposite extreme, we saw the current fad
against Western medicine with a sudden abundance of
people calling themselves healers. Healing was being reduced to a technique of visualizing problems going away.
Almost nowhere in those visualizations was there mention
of a higher power or presence. All too often, instead of
letting the doctor cut the illness out, people were letting
their minds chop up and discard the disease. No one
seemed to be talking about loving the illness, as Genny
felt compelled to do. In this process people could learn
why they decided against their natural wholeness in the
first place. For Genny illness served some purpose other
than for our minds to try to disregard it.

One evening we went to visit a spiritual group. The
people were divided into pairs, with everyone doing laying
on of hands. The leader announced, "Everyone is a healer."
It felt like we were in a room with twenty beginners
playing the piano at the same time. What was disturbing
to us was that no one seemed to feel the energy. In our
society, a concert pianist has the gift of talent and has
spent years of discipline before performing. But so many
of the people we met were all ready to put out a shingle
and practice healing after only learning one particular
technique.

Feeling little legitimate ground prepared for her,
Genny continually had to prepare her own. We both wanted
to travel and live in a culture in which acceptance of
other states of consciousness was a natural way of life. We
yearned to work with and learn from teachers who did
not merely teach techniques, but who had gone through
their own personal hell and found heaven within. We
dreamed of living with teachers who lived what they taught.

Genny was exploding with all the energy she was
opening to. She knew her doubts and judgments were
creating the demons that came to her. She had to make

friends with these feelings. She had to connect over and over again with her own perfection. The *Course* said:

> *"When a mind has only light, it knows only light. It's own radiance shines all round it, and extends out into the darkness of other minds, transforming them into majesty."*[32] T - 127

Understanding what these words meant, and knowing the meaning of the *Course* was not always as easy.

One day I came home and found Genny sitting on the bathroom floor yelling and screaming, "Get out! Get out! Leave me alone! Leave! Leave!" She was motioning towards one corner where she felt demons hovering over her. "Leave!" she said. "Go somewhere where you can serve some purpose. Go away! Go into the clouds. Make it rain!" Then she counseled them, "Until you can come in some form that I can learn from, go!"

Until they could do that, she ordered them to go away. It was like a primal scene. But the feelings were not from the past, but right in the moment. There were demons right there in our bathroom. Suddenly, all my experience with people crying and screaming came back to me. Genny's extremes, as she pounded the floor, did not scare me. I sat down on the floor with her. "Where was this path taking us," I thought.

It was fall, and the sky had been clear every day because of the long drought. When Genny had sent the demons fully away, we stepped out onto the street to find a single, dark cloud overhead, and as we watched, the rain began to splatter around us. My mind tried desperately to convince myself that it was only a strange coincidence. But something in me knew better. At that moment both of us began to have a much greater respect for the power of the energy we were dealing with.

Genny was going through heaven and hell, and there was no one who could know what it all meant. Her old friends saw her as a former flight attendant. Her new friends saw her training to be a healer, with all the usual skepticism and judgments such activity arouses in people. She felt so alone. She couldn't understand how God could feel so close at one moment and only a short time later leave her feeling so abandoned.

Her energy was like a teeter-totter, sitting balanced between heaven and earth being a fine movement to master. I could see the extremes of her behavior and mental states slowly reaching a balance. I trusted what was happening for her, and I was dealing with my own fears. I had to confront the part of me that was jealous. I had been through therapy and many experiences, but Genny, without going through a day of therapy in her life, was going head first into the midst of her monsters. I felt mine still lurking about, even more menacing.

I had to admit that physical illness scared me. In spite of all my training with Doris, my hands still did not respond to the energy. I knew I was holding back. My mind tried to figure out how healing worked. I knew stress was the cause of most disease. But the truth I was discovering about myself was so much greater. I was not ready to surrender to loving someone who was ill and appeared out of control. I had not found the same capacity that came so naturally to Genny. My formal schooling in psychology and the time I spent in personal therapy could not compare to the effects of Genny's honesty and purity, which reached out to the same innocence in many people.

I felt trapped between my past identity as a psychologist and my new perception about our true nature. My training as a therapist was to help people identify and acknowledge the source of their pain. Spiritually, I was seeing that ultimately the pain did not exist. Illness is only a test to learn from, while healing serves to reaffirm the part of us which is well. Perhaps to someone else the differences would be small. But for me, somehow, my whole view of myself was at stake. After years of working in psychology, I'd seen the need to help people recognize the feelings behind their behavior and defenses. The emphasis on feeling was so important. Now I knew that feelings are not ends in themselves, but merely vehicles to bring one closer to one's spirit. Getting angry or crying is not the resolution but is sometimes necessary before forgiving and finding inner peace. How much useless energy is spent searching for and confronting feelings, when the real hunger is left unrecognized and unsatisfied? It was beginning to be so clear to me why relationships are confused, why personalities are in conflict. We look everywhere for the answers, instead of seeking something much more pure and infinite, something within us. After all my years in school, and involvement in my own therapy and training, I was beginning to realize that knowing God is the real source of my happiness, and the ramifications of that realization scared me to death!

God is such an outcast in our society. To align myself with something which is supremely gentle and subtle, all knowing and purposeful, was like asking the impossible from myself.

Everything in my personal history, education, and culture was saying I was a fool for believing I could accept dependence upon something supposedly greater than myself. But that was exactly what Genny and I were doing. How else could we explain the forces which were moving in our lives? How else could we explain all the coincidences, the dreams, the visions? How else could we make sense of our meeting, and our growing relationship? Who else but God could arrange such a union?

I knew the answer, and I hated knowing it. I felt trapped by it. Knowing the answer forced me into a new world because it was true. A part of my being felt dragged against my will, and another part was desperately hungry for more. I tried to hide from the judgments I had always made about religious people. Genny, meanwhile, hated all the prejudicial benefits of my old identity. She was especially irked when people were being impressed by me simply because I was a male and had a degree. Both of us felt we were taking on new identities, identities which left us vulnerable and unacknowledged. The internal storm which had been shaping the new identities went unnoticed by the world. We were afraid of drowning, yet we knew that we had to dive further into the feminine within us, the intuitive, the unknown. It was only from there that we would be realized.

We began to realize why Doris so intensely disliked being put on a pedestal, for it made her and her own surrender different from others. We could also understand why she hated the medical authorities for not seeing her as an equal, when the results of her work showed that she was their equal in so many ways. Doris was a master of life's mystery. She had fully opened up to the unknown and found incredible depths of knowing. She taught from her own mortality and capacity to love. Healing in our culture seemed so much more about technology than about the importance of faith and trust, which is what we were learning.

Our quiet little cottage was the perfect place for us to isolate our inner dramas of conflict, keeping it within the walls of our relationship. The tempo of our lives was changing again. We had become volunteers at a unique center working with children who had cancer. Our lives were filled with clients and appointments. We recognized the wisdom of the Divine Protection which had not allowed us to have our dream house in Bolinas. Living on the other side of the mountain would have prevented many of the opportunities which were now coming to us. We thanked God for saving us from having to commute over the mountain every day. After autumn slipped into winter, we again called our New York publisher. We finally reached the editor, who had previously expressed interest in our book. She picked up the phone and said, "Oh, I've been meaning to call you. We're going with the book. If all goes well, it should be out by next summer."

I was stunned. As I thanked her and hung up the phone, a hundred questions came into my mind. But all I could do was tell Genny, and dance around the house. *Hugs & Kisses* was to be a book! For some reason, the acceptance of our book gave legitimacy to our entire lives. We realized that one really could make a living from hugging and kissing, that love really does have a place in this world. We prepared a special picnic and went to the top of Mt. Tamalpais for a feast and ritual of deep thankfulness.

It wasn't long before Doris was in town again. The first night she stayed with us, I dreamed that Genny was going out with another man. The same night Genny dreamed I was with another woman. It was "only" a dream, but we were both still angry when we reported our feelings to Doris the next morning. She laughed and said, "I programmed your dreams, but it's up to you to look at the jealousy which is running just beneath the surface."

Doris was in California because she, Genny, and I were to do a workshop on healing. It was to be held at the ranch where Doris and I had met several years ago. As we drove to the ranch, I thought of that meeting, and the impact this woman had had on my life. Never would I have imagined that someday I would be returning to work with Doris.

The workshop began smoothly, with the three of us explaining our work together. During the break, Doris went off alone to consult with her guides about programming new behavior for many of us. She announced to everyone, "Of course, you will not do something against your will, but if you feel an urge to try something new, try it!"

At dinner I was going through the buffet line, when I found myself reaching for the chicken and putting two pieces on my plate. This was strange, because I had been a vegetarian for years. As we sat down Doris smiled and said, "Try it."

Doris eats everything. I ate the chicken and enjoyed it. I realized that the rules my mind was making for my body denied my changing needs and desires in the moment. In spite of the many reasons I had for not eating meat, by putting myself on such a diet I was avoiding the responsibility of listening to what my body really wanted. Disciplines of any kind can be counter productive if they perpetuate conflict within us. Sooner or later our "shoulds" and our desires have to be reconciled.

That night Doris attempted to appear in the dreams of the twelve people in our group. The next morning she pointed out the two who wouldn't accept her. To one she said, "You were awake half the night and I got tired of waiting for you to go to sleep." To the second person she said, "You just said 'no' when I asked permission of your guides to enter."

Doris explained spirit guides. She told us that we all have these guides. Who they are is determined by the degree of our spiritual progress. They can be deceased family and friends, or spiritual teachers and masters. At any given time, we have anywhere from one guide to twenty or even thirty. Doris told the story of visiting a scientist who was working alone in his lab. Doris felt the lab crammed with helpers, spirits from the other side, who were there as his assistants. It didn't matter that he didn't consciously believe in spirits.

Before Doris returned to Alaska, Genny had a dream about her. In the dream, Doris was in a hospital, dying, and Genny was bringing flowers. They were hugging and saying goodbye. The next morning she told Doris the dream. Doris nodded. "The time is nearing," she said. "Our relationship is indeed changing, and I will no longer be your teacher. You are ready to go on."

We understood what was happening, but we didn't want it to be so definite, so permanent. Our relationship with Doris was changing dramatically. There was no contact between us for many months.

Chapter Six

I proposed to Genny in a Chinese restaurant. I had been thinking about it all day. We were beginning the meal when I asked her, "Would you—will you marry me?"

She thought about it as she finished eating her egg roll. Each bite seemed to last a full minute. She laid her fork down, wiped her mouth, and staring at her tea cup answered, "Yes . . . Yes."

As a startled waiter watched us, we jumped up, hugged and kissed and danced around our table. When I told him the goods news, he abandoned his professional detachment, and joined us in our happy excitement. Not many proposals had taken place in his small restaurant.

It had been over a year since we had met. I had had the vision that we were to be married in the fall. Well, one fall had passed and it was now spring. It would be fall again before we had everything arranged. In my vision it had been an outdoor wedding, and Genny had always had the same picture. Our individual desires to have an informal wedding, like so many other details in our lives, were the same.

Genny and I teased each other. We recalled our first days together. I thought she had seduced me first, but of course she insisted it was the other way around.

We both remembered our first days together as we each wanted to. So much had happened since our days of innocence, our days of hiking and exploring Germany and Switzerland. Now we were in the midst of our new work and life together. We had so much in common. Genny would say that she wasn't certain if we enjoyed the same food, activities, and days with one another because we really had so much in common or because we had spent so much time together. Since we had been two very independent people when we met, I was amazed at the evolution of our relationship. From the time Genny had joined me in Europe, we had not been apart for more than a few hours. Without feeling the need to push or pull each other, it was so easy and natural to spend so much time together. Our major everyday difference was that she enjoyed shopping, which bored me completely. I would usually wander through the local bookstore until she returned.

Our relationship was unlike anything we had experienced with other people. Almost from the beginning, there had been none of the usual drama and fear of rejection. We knew we were falling in love with God as much as we were falling in love with each other. The changing winds of the unknown were the source of our excitement, which included the awe, and feelings of utter insanity, trusting in something so unbelievable. Our affair was not about us as two personalities. We did not look for validation of our love affair in the details of our common interests and desires. We found it in the depths of our individual commitments to unravel our greater purpose, and to help each other reveal that purpose.

The *Course* said:

> *"In reality you are perfectly unaffected by all expressions of lack of love. These can be from yourself and others, from yourself to others, or from*

*others to you. Peace is an attribute in you. You
cannot find it outside."*[33]

It was clear that when either one of us was really
upset with the other, we were only fighting with our
individual selves. Because we knew this, we had an extraordinary amount of trust in each other. We had that
extraordinary amount of faith in our relationship because
of the constant stream of small signs, or miracles, as we
called them, that continued to open new paths for us. Our
occasional fights were attempts to convince each other
that our worries and fears were real. Occasionally we
were successful. But as soon as one of us remembered the
Holy Spirit, the other would realize that the anger and
hostility was really our resistance, our fear of letting go
some more and trusting.

The basic trap we would try to pull one another
into was: "Can't you see I'm miserable? Don't you care?
Can't you see our lives aren't working?" Or in other words,
"Won't you join me in my resistance and my fear of
having to surrender and surrender and trust and trust?
Won't you join me in this bottomless pit that I'm jumping
into?"

By one of us refusing to jump in with the other at
those moments, Genny or I became conscious that we
were choosing to jump and we were not just being forced
into the pit against our will.

For us it was a new kind of a relationship. We had
always thought our differences should be talked out and
settled between us. Now we were also learning that, more
often than not, our differences were not between each
other but that each of us was struggling with our own
path. We would joke with friends, trying to explain our
relationship as basically a *ménage à trois*, Bruce, Genny,
and our never ending adventure with the Holy Spirit.

Our lifestyle, meanwhile, was becoming so whole-
some that it almost frightened us. Genny had given up
smoking long before. Recently she felt the effects of coffee
and wine either speeding her up or making her dizzy. She

gave them up too. I also found that I no longer wanted alcohol or marijuana. The extremes of our life had disappeared, so that we could more completely enjoy our days and meditations. We had not consciously given up staying out all night, along with our other reckless youthful passions. They were simply no longer satisfying in comparison to what we were now enjoying.

Oftentimes, during our lovemaking, we would literally see angels. At other times, sex was simply the enjoyment of our physical natures. Our physical and emotional compatibility were not standards to judge our relationship. It was hard to verbalize the alchemy that brought us together and continued to mystify us, blasting through our normal personalities instead of bringing them together. We had to be open for surprises in our everyday moods and feelings. Fortunately, something greater was always there, holding us and our relationship. Without that something, our fears and periodic fits of anger would have separated us long ago. Between Genny's storms I saw the part of her that was giving, giving, more and more. Genny said that between my occasional fits of desperation and hopelessness, a light and caring peacefulness was emerging and constantly expanding. Forgiveness had taken us both to new and incredible depths of openness. We were gradually seeing that there was something much more basic and fundamental which would tie the bow of marriage for us.

The *Course* said:

> *"The grace of God rests gently on forgiving eyes, and everything they look on speaks of Him to the beholder. He can see no evil, nothing in the world to fear, and no one who is different from himself."* [34]

When one of us was paralyzed with fear, the other did not need to jump in as well, making it more real. We jut waited for each other, and learned various ways to be unconditionally supportive. We were learning to live in the moment with each other.

The *Course* said:

> *"Deep within you is everything that is perfect, ready to radiate through you and out into the world."*[35]

It was right for us to get married because, as partners, we had common beliefs. Our hearts went out to couples who did not mutually feel, as the *Course* said:

> *"The peace of God is my one goal; the air of all my living here, the end I seek, my purpose and my function and my life."*[36]

If both partners didn't care about inner peace, the relationship could still work. But when one partner was falling in love with God, and the other was oblivious to his/her changes, the pain and the separateness seemed so hopeless.

We knew a beautiful woman who began having glorious visions of a divine Master coming to her and holding her. Her husband couldn't understand the effects of the sudden new love she was feeling, and believed that she was secretly seeing another man. She had to learn to depend more and more on her spiritual self to give her the strength to forgive and love her partner, even when he ridiculed her spiritual journey. Her strength in transforming the relationship earned our awe and respect. She often wanted to leave, and sometimes she did. But she returned to her family each time, with renewed faith.

Working with couples became part of our best work. We saw in them the aspects of ourselves which were skeptical and afraid of risking more and compromising less. We saw the part of us that was afraid of opening up to more love. And we saw the parts of ourselves that wanted to struggle, to hold on tighter and tighter to what we had. When two people did let go of their need for each other to be different and found, instead, that what they wanted was inside of themselves, the transformation was beautiful. We could see it in their faces. Trust seemed, literally, to restore relationships.

In a few more months it would be a year since our return from Europe. Neither of us had had a normal job in that time. Genny had some benefits due her from the airline. While she worked with Greg, she gained experience but no income. I had seen a few clients who had heard of my work as a therapist. We were expecting our advance from *Hugs & Kisses* to arrive soon. A check for $2,500 was expected any day. "How," we asked ourselves, "did we ever survive all these months?" *Hugs & Kisses* was the carrot that gave us the faith to keep moving in the direction we wanted. It was amazing how, so many times, at the last moment, the money came in from the least expected directions.

In the past, we would have worked at regular jobs to earn our money and attempted to pursue our personal directions in whatever time was left over. That way would have left us personally unsatisfied and probably still concerned with lack of finances. During this year, we were discovering that love could provide security much greater than we ever imagined. But how far could we trust it? Significantly, the arrival of our first check for *Hugs & Kisses* came when we were asking that question the most.

Not long before, Genny had reached the peak of her crisis. Her doubts and her faith were all on the surface. She was climbing and pounding an invisible wall inside her, wanting to know what was on the other side. Where was all this torment and energy leading to? She was tired of living in the moment, one day at a time, tired of always trying to trust. In the midst of this struggle, Greg told her to take time for herself and meditate, and truly ask herself what being a healer meant to her. She would be gone for hours. She spent time walking on the beach and watching the ocean. She would ask herself questions. "Did she really want a life full of Spirit, which included incredible risks and feelings that she didn't belong in this world? How committed was she? How strong was the voice that urged her to return to being just a 'normal person,' whatever that was?" She asked for help.

Genny came home looking so different. I had never seen her so relaxed. Her face was glowing when she told me what had happened. She had seen Christ, and had felt such love and peace and strength flowing from Him as He sat with her beside the ocean. All He wanted to do was to take her problems and love her. He asked her, "Are you willing to give up your problems for me?"

As her visions continued, her serenity grew all week.

My heart was awakened by the transformation that she was undergoing. My Jewish background, including the ingrained hostility about Jesus, was over-ruled by the genuineness of Genny's joy. There was no way I could judge her. I could only ask myself, "Why was I unable to surrender and feel? What prevented me from opening my heart and feeling the love that she felt? Why was my mind raging with the religious wars of my ancestors?" I, too, asked for help. I knew my fears were born out of the history of injustice towards the Jewish people. But for how long will we continue to see ourselves as separate? For how long will we refuse to see that every man is a Christian and a Jew, a Hindu and a Moslem? Everything Genny and I were growing into was reinforcing a belief that we had been brought together as Christian and Jew to remind people that there is only one God, no matter how many different religions there are. I knew also that my intellectual debate was really a facade, covering something deeper. Was I willing to surrender, as Genny had done? Was I willing to really give up my need to control, to be in charge? That part of me that was taught that being a male meant being aggressive and assuming responsibility for a family was seeking help as well.

That week Genny dreamt about saying goodbye to Greg, as she had dreamt before about Doris. She had found, and now knew without question, that her real teacher was within her. When she told me the dream, we both instantly knew its meaning. But again, we didn't want it to be so definite, so permanent. Genny talked to

Greg. They decided it was time for her to work on her own. Her next question was how would anyone discover that she was a healer? She was clear about her intention and the way in which she would serve. But she did not know how she would begin her service.

The first night after making the decision, Genny fretted. She was feeling sorry for herself and was skeptical that all of this would really work out. The phone rang, and I answered it. A woman wanted to speak with Genny. Genny took the phone. Standing close by I could hear the woman saying, "I understand that you do healing work. I have cancer. Can you help me?"

Genny's face, at that moment, was priceless. She was excited and nervous. This was her first client. The irony is that that particular person, because of some mixup in her calendar, never actually came in for a session. Her phone call, however, was just what Genny needed. Within days, others were also calling, and coming.

Within several months, we began working together. The combination of my counseling skills and her loving hands was good for both of us. Genny was growing accustomed to letting her hands talk to, and touch, the body of each of the clients. Invariably, the clients were amazed that she was touching them just where they felt they needed to be touched at specific moments in the session. I would meditate with her, asking to see God in the healing. Often, visions or personal words for the client would come to me. This was my opportunity to ask if my hands could also be used as instruments. Sometimes I felt energy in them. Sometimes when I felt them getting warmer and warmer, I would also use them. But there was a part of me which was still not at ease.

Our relationship with a client began the moment he called. After taking his name and setting a time for an appointment, we would sit down and meditate. In our meditations we would ask how we could serve this person. Afterwards, we would compare notes to see if we received the same information regarding his problem and his particular need for healing. Genny and I used this time to train each other.

People came under all sorts of circumstances. Some people came by themselves. Often, people brought hesitant partners or friends, for them to "try it." We learned to ask permission of their guides or their higher selves before channeling healing. We knew that it was not our personal energy being used during the healing. We were just there to help the person experience that part of himself which was much greater than his current conflict or illness.

Because of this, each session was dramatically different. Some people would recognize the presence of lost loved ones. Some would see angels, while others would experience a calmness and a sense of well-being, knowing that everything really was all right! What we called God was an experience, a vision, or a feeling which came for each person in a way that he was ready to receive it. What was beautiful was recognizing that God loved everyone unconditionally, regardless of one's prejudices or limits in the way one would receive His embrace. Of course that was our goal. No matter what appeared to be wrong, we knew the truth, that in some place in their being they were indeed all right.

At times, however, we were shocked by the misery that some people had in their lives. We were learning that people never had a trauma or crisis that they could not handle at some level. There were many times we could not imagine wearing the shoes of those who came to us. But people told us that they could not imagine leading the life we were living, with no normal means of security. We had to go beyond our judgments. It was clear, however, that the deeper people proceeded into their darkness, the more their spirit was able to risk searching for its own light. We may all be created equal, but many people we worked with, people who experienced so much tragedy, had spiritual capacities much greater than we had ever known existed. Their lives required a powerful faith in action simply to get through each day.

Some people weren't sure if they should return to a

spiritual healer for more treatments. Sometimes, the answer was obvious. At other times we told them to check out how they felt. If they found a dramatic change, for the better or worse, taking place in the following seventy-two hours, we felt the healing was successful. If a lot of pain surfaced, that usually meant that previously blocked areas were now loosening, and feeling was being restored.

The problem of money never seemed to be completely answered. Sometimes we felt we shouldn't charge for our work. We felt that since we had been given these gifts freely, they should be given to others freely also. There were people who had such high altruistic standards for healers, expecting our services to be free, yet they wouldn't think twice about paying the high fees of therapists and doctors. Yet we asked, "How are we going to make a living?"

For awhile we left the donation up to our clients. After a healing, we felt so high that it didn't seem to matter. But at the end of a day, when we would look in our little donations box, the doubts came. "How could we survive on this?" we wondered. So we began asking for a specified donation based on a sliding scale. We didn't want to turn people away because they couldn't afford it. Yet, very often it seemed that when people did pay something, they truly valued the work. We wanted everyone to pay what they could. Regardless which system we tried, God provided us with what we needed—maybe not what we wanted at the time, but we were consistently taken care of.

Before a client left, we would give him a meditation, which had come intuitively, for him to try during the week for five minutes twice a day. Usually it was similar to asking him to imagine the highest image of love or light that was real for him. Then he was asked to feel the experience of that image, both around and within him, while, at the same time, surrendering any fears and doubts in his life to that feeling. It was not important exactly what the image was. The experience is what counted.

These meditations seemed to continue the experience of healing which was begun during our sessions.

So often meditation was a chore for people, a routine during which some found themselves falling asleep and which others made into a discipline, full of difficulties and obstacles. Many people we met were much more connected to their mantra, the picture of their teacher, yoga exercises, or some technique, than simply using some time during the day as a time to receive. We had to practice not judging other people's ways even though to us they seemed so often full of unnecessary ritual or self-examination.

The *Course* said:

> *"Teach no one that he is what you would not want to be. Your brother is the mirror in which you see the image of yourself."*[37]

No matter how difficult someone's path appeared to be, it felt like an amplification of something we were learning ourselves. Together we were working to see God in our midst.

The *Course* said:

> *"There is no veil the love of God in us together cannot lift. The way to truth is open."*[38]

Our work led us to see that whether the problem presented was emotional or physical, it was only a veil. Our primary goal was to experience the peace on the other side. The problem was secondary, at least for us, if not always for the clients also. During sessions, we practiced remembering from the *Course:*

> *"Now is the closest approximation of eternity that this world offers. It is in the reality of now, without past or future, that the beginning of the appreciation of eternity lies."*[39]

*   *   *

The brief time we spent with each client and God was timeless. Nothing else mattered but that feeling of being an empty cup one moment, full the next, sharing it and feeling it received.

Often, before going to bed at night, we would watch the sunset splash its colors all over our living room, and we would read the *Course* once again before going to sleep:

> *"The extension of the Holy Spirit's purpose from your relationship to others, to bring them gently in, will quietly extend to every aspect of your lives, surrounding both of you with glowing happiness and the calm awareness of complete protection. And you will carry its message of love and safety and freedom to everyone who draws nigh unto your temple, where healing waits for him."*[40]

Our work was giving our relationship more and more purpose. Our marriage was to be more than a ceremony bringing the two of us together. It seemed that it would signify our commitment to include others in the love we were discovering.

We heard from Doris again, for the first time in many months. She was coming down from Alaska to attend a convention in Las Vegas. We had written her to ask her to officiate with Greg at our wedding. We needed to spend some time with her to make plans for the ceremony. Her guides had told her that we should go along on her trip to Nevada. We didn't feel that we needed to spend that much time with her, but we didn't want to oppose her guides either. So, we went. The meetings she attended were of no interest to us, so we used the opportunity to enjoy the sun and the slot machines. I also enjoyed thinking that maybe God wanted us to come to Las Vegas, so we could turn a dollar investment into a treasure. Then we wouldn't ever have to worry about money again. With Genny and Doris being such great psychics, I thought we should win a fortune. We didn't. That wasn't how the

Holy Spirit worked, at least for us. We knew that first we had to learn not to worry. Then the money would be provided. Well, we thought, maybe we were sent here simply to relax and have a good time.

We were on our way to the airport for our return flight to San Francisco, when Doris told me to change our reservations. We were to fly to Sacramento instead. When we landed, she told me to rent a car while she made a phone call. As we were loading the car, she explained that her guides had told her early that day to introduce us to a couple who lived north of Sacramento. She wasn't exactly certain why, but she knew it would all work out. She had just called them and they were excited about our coming. As soon as we'd heard that we were driving to a town called Paradise, it sounded more interesting.

Doris had met Jennie briefly at a workshop a couple of years before, but had not been in touch since. Jennie and Cal were a joyous older couple. The instant we met them, we felt we were with family.

We immediately became close friends and adopted Jennie and Cal as our California parents. They had never had children, so the adoption was just perfect for all of us. Thanks to Doris, we were to be close friends and family for many years to come, but it was the first and last time Doris visited them.

We traveled up to Paradise every few months. Jennie had been involved with metaphysics for over thirty years. She had weekly meetings with her "girls" (most of whom were in their sixties or older). They meditated, worked with sacred readings which had been handed down for dozens of generations, and practiced distant healing. Being with Jennie and her "girls" was truly cleansing and helped to reinforce our own work. At their meetings, they would turn the lights down low, and each woman would meditate. The room would fill with the softest, yet most powerful, energy. As I would look around the room, the women seemed to have changed into monks, clothed in dark robes. Frequently a spirit of a lion appeared in the center of the circle. After a while, when several people had acknowledged they could see it, the lion would dissolve into a column of light. The women would then get down to the business of sending healing to the people on their lists. Afterwards, everyone would gossip and make small talk, eating cake and drinking coffee, as if they had just completed playing a hand of cards. All of the ladies loved us, and we loved all the attention. Paradise was exactly the second home we needed.

Our client load was always fluctuating. More and more people were coming to us because they had heard about the results of the healings we were doing. But because we saw most people only once, or just a few times, there was a big turnover. We had been certain that if we were going to be of help, a healing would have to happen quickly. On the other hand, since our goal was not only to heal the current ailment, but to lead people into their own increased spiritual awareness, it felt appropriate for some people to stay and study with us. As long as we were busy, we felt great! We felt that we were on course, full of purpose. But sometimes, when we would go through an inactive period, a "dry spell," we would get overwhelmed by a feeling of panic. Only after going through many separate times of our work slowing down and picking up again did we begin to face our free time with less fear. We were gradually beginning to enjoy each free time as a spiritual vacation.

We were in the middle of one such "dry spell," when a small cottage right next door became available. We thought it would be ideal as an office for us to see our clients. But could we afford it? Were we taking on too much? At that point, we had seen almost no clients for two weeks. Considering practicalities, it was foolish to rent another building. We drove up to Jennie's, as we often did when we were confronting such decisions. Her support, along with the time away from our everyday lives, usually allowed us to find the answer.

This time, however, we were still in conflict. Something within us said, "Of course. Rent the cottage. It is being presented to you." Then we thought, "We're already using our house; the Center with children with cancer lets us use their building; and another friend has a room we could use." But the other voice persisted. "Take it." How could we? We didn't have the money for first and last month's rent. We asked for a clearer sign and drove back home still feeling unresolved about the whole thing.

The first few hours home were busy returning phone calls and going through the mail. I opened a letter from the bank. It was a very strange notice; a deposit had been made to our account, a deposit of exactly the amount we needed to rent the office. The coincidence was mind-boggling. We called the bank right away to see if it was a mistake. They checked . . . "No, we assure you the deposit is legitimate." We immediately put the money to its divinely intended use and rented the cottage.

Six weeks later we were notified that the bank had indeed made a mistake. We gave thanks in our meditations for the forced loan. We also asked for forgiveness for needing so many signs, for needing almost constant proof that something greater was taking care of us. Why couldn't we simply accept God's love for itself? As a couple, we rarely challenged each other to prove our affections. But we often seemed to be testing God, like two children constantly running back to see if He was still there.

We had to admit that every time He was there for us, waiting with open arms. Perhaps our difficulty came because the answers didn't reveal themselves to us in the ways we expected them to. Sometimes it felt as if we were falling for a long time before landing in the net. But we were never let down when we trusted. We were increasingly discovering a universal order that overwhelmed us. Learning to live in the unknown, in the fourth dimension, was to trust that it would be the source of everything, including our very livelihood. The purposefulness of that force was reaching down and touching us with increased frequency. The fourth dimension made so much sense out of the chaos in the first three dimensions. In this dimension, I could see so easily how time and space could be manipulated.

Our wedding was now upon us. It was going to be a three day celebration of the reality of the fourth dimension fully and powerfully at work in our lives. All the people we felt closest to were there. The ranch where it had all begun when I met Doris, and Michael and Marsha, who introduced me to Genny, was the perfect place for the celebration. The people invited were from all walks of life, but few were accustomed to seeing a marriage performed by a shaman and a healer. But everyone was in love with love as much as we were. As in my original vision, my grandmother was there enjoying herself. Everyone surrendered to experiencing something new and different, and allowed themselves to enjoy being at the ranch together. Even though the long drought had left everything parched, with few flowers or plants in bloom, the heat of the sun and the swimming pools kept all of us happy.

The ceremony combined tradition with shamanistic ritual. We had included the beauty of the wedding march, played by a flutist, and the special blessings of our spiritual teachers, Doris and Greg, in our wedding vows. It felt that our marriage was so much more than a union of two people. We felt we were witnessing the forces of heaven and earth coming together. And we were honored to be present at this event.

Genny had made me a wedding shirt. In search for her own dress, Genny met a stranger—an angel—in a downtown store who, after finding out what she was looking for, whisked her away to a seamstress. Together they designed the perfect angel dress with flowing sleeves that went nearly to the ground. In the back, literally a hundred buttons pulled the yards and yards of white silk into a flowing pattern which seemed to hold Genny above the earth.

All the details had fallen into their divinely ordered place. While we were in Europe, in the beginning, we had felt that the world was cheering for us, and we were cheering the world. That day we celebrated, again feeling the harmony all around us.

A friend provided us with a cabin in Tahoe to retreat to after the weekend. In my Fiat convertible, trailing tin cans, we stopped on the way at a drive-in for root beer and french fries. When we finally arrived at the cabin we could see it had been closed up for months. The rooms smelled very stale. We were too tired to bother cleaning up, so we went to bed.

Minutes later, Genny was tossing in her sleep. At the same time, I was having a dream that Doris appeared at the front door telling us to be careful because the house was possessed. Together we tried to exorcise the lower spirits. We were failing when Genny woke me up. The house had a chill in it, and we were both frightened. Genny had just dreamed that something was holding her down and she couldn't move her hands.

The house was strangely quiet. What should we do? We couldn't sleep here. It was late, and there was nowhere else to go. Genny picked up her wedding bouquet and some salt. I rummaged in our bags until I found our Bible. Half-naked, we walked from room to room, calling upon all the love we felt at our wedding to be with us now, to fill up the cabin. We felt the tears of joy, the hugs, and so many of the small kind touches once again with us. We felt the unwanted energy, the lost spirits who had hung around in the house, leave each room as we entered. We lit a candle and returned to bed. This time we felt the warmth and love, the golden moments of the last few days tucking us in.

Chapter Seven

Doris met us in Tahoe for a couple of days while we were still on our honeymoon. After our wedding she had visited a scientist who was doing very technical cancer research. Perhaps because of the continued harassment she received from Alaskan authorities for practicing medicine without a license, Doris had become a constant student. In cancer research she had been involved with laetrile, B12, and other less-known approaches. She had worked with chiropractors and other body specialists to learn about their latest techniques. She had also been expanding her ever-growing awareness of herbs with the Alaskan natives. She flew to England and earned her master's degree from one of the most advanced acupuncture clinics. Through the university system, she received her Ph.D., in religion. The day that she met us in Tahoe, Doris casually mentioned the story of how she got a medical degree from the University of Mexico. "Before I was to leave Ecuador permanently, I commuted to Mexico City. There I had the opportunity to study and take a licensing exam. The final medical boards were in German, however. And I didn't speak any German. But my guides assured me that they would help me. I felt strongly that the M.D. certificate would be important some day along the way. Anyway, under the guidance of my guides, I did remarkably well on the exam."

For some reason, never entirely clear to me, having the Mexican medical license never got the authorities off Doris' back. On at least two occasions, the local medical association had arranged for her to be indicted and jailed. Doris had found her own place in the battle between native traditions and the Western influences in Alaska. One of the greatest problems they were having had to do with the fact that before Western doctors came, the natives practiced mental birth control. It was very important not to become pregnant during certain months of the year, so that the baby would not be born in the winter, as this usually meant certain death because of the extreme cold. But since the natives had opened up to Western medicine and doctors had placed doubts in their minds about mental birth control, what was once a sound and a virtually 100-percent-effective system was now falling apart. The natives had given up their firm belief in controlling their own bodies and began using the pill and other birth control devices, which meant that babies were now being born in the midst of winter.

As I listened to more of Doris' stories, I began to see how she was a symbol of a dying way of life. And as she fought back, to be an equal in degrees and influence, I couldn't help but feel her spirit saddened. I felt she was losing a precious part of herself in her struggle for survival.

We talked and took long walks around the lake and through the woods. Genny and I could feel how lonely Doris was. The man who had nursed her back to health and guided her through the rain forests and jungles of Ecuador, one day, not too long after their move to Alaska, walked outdoors during a heavy winter storm and never came back. He was later found, his body was frozen. He had been sitting on a log, resting. Several hundred miles away, when the headmaster walked into her children's classroom to announce the news, before anything was said Doris' oldest boy stood up and said, "I know. My father is dead."

It was clear that all the education and training Doris had since accomplished could not fill up the loss she had felt. She was very proud. But underneath we felt an innocence which so deserved to be loved. We felt guilty with the thought that maybe all the love at our wedding only made her feelings sharper and more difficult. All the spirit at her command could not, or at least had not, healed the human love which she was missing.

We talked about men and their need to feel superior. It would take a rare man these days to match up to Doris or to not be threatened by her. The differences in rules for men and women in our culture seemed bizarre to her and deeply upset her. Doris, with all of her experiences, was over-qualified for many things, but most of all for romance. She had thought about moving down to the mainland and living in California. But the callousness of our culture was too dramatic. She needed the wilderness and space of Alaska.

When we said goodbye to Doris at the Reno airport, it was the only sad farewell I could remember. At the time, we didn't know, consciously, that it would be our last time together for a long, long time, if ever. I had never really expressed to Doris how much she had given to me, with her soft center, her endless patience, and her love, for which I am always thankful. Doris rescued me from myself at a time in my life when I most needed it. I guess she knows that now.

We returned home really appreciating the little cottage which had come to us, because suddenly an abundance of people were calling. Our cottage had become a hub for people with all kinds of needs. Common threads of feeling unworthy of love often emerged from our sessions. Many of our clients had been giving to others all their lives, but they had never learned that true giving only comes from the heart. And with the heart, giving and receiving are the same. Most of them felt that they had never been truly given to without some conditions. They had always had to do something for love. Illness was their test in how far the body would go in a cry for love.

It was a beautiful setting in which we helped people to embrace themselves exactly as they were. The work was more non-verbal than intellectual. Our goal was always becoming clearer—to help others to feel their spirit, which was already perfect and whole.

One person we were seeing frequently had symptoms of multiple sclerosis. We say symptoms, because as soon as the illness is confirmed, people often begin living out the sentence of the disease which by reputation follows a particular course. Having the label of such an illness so often puts people in a category which can become a prison. This woman was in such a prison. More crippling than the discomfort of her current numbness were her fears of eventually becoming much worse. In addition, she was trying to complete college. It was important to her—too important. Although we supported her, at times her hands refused to cooperate. She cursed them, and then tried to love them. We saw her hands as little fairies that were so light, and each finger was a finger of an angel. Her hands could not perform what was not in tune with their sensitivity. They would rather create fine delicate miniature drawings than type a dissertation. The conflict was more complex. But simply stated, the angel in her was in conflict with all her doubts and needs for recognition. When we worked, we felt the part of her which truly was an angel, and we all cried. But in this world there was no such recognition.

There was another woman who had severe kidney problems, along with many other physical difficulties. She had to be hooked up to a dialysis machine several times a week. She was always worrying about her children, who were rebelling against her denial of her life-threatening situation. She worried about her husband and his feelings of being trapped in caring for her. She was also preoccupied with her brother, who was also very ill. No matter how much love she received during the healing, we couldn't influence her attitudes of self-sacrifice and guilt and her tendency to avoid her own needs. We watched her sink in and out of the clutches of darkness, the likes of which we have never seen. Our respect for her spirit and strength grew and grew.

Some days, after a full schedule of seeing clients, we would take their inner struggles home with us. Sometimes we would find ourselves arguing about an unresolved conflict that didn't belong to us. After we began to realize what we were doing, we decided that it was important to take time to sit in prayer before and after each session. At these times we would once again affirm the presence of God within each person. We did not want to leave identifying people with their problems but remembering the part of them which was always much greater.

The *Course* said that illness is a defense against the truth. Some religious groups we met seemed to say that illness does not exist. Many of the New Thought groups have similar philosophies, but we feel that the challenge is for people to actually see that their illness is a defense against the truth of their inner beauty and perfection. Then we have a personal experience instead of an intellectual attitude, which we found people trying to force themselves to accept. As Western medicine denied the emotional and spiritual factors in illness, some people involved in alternative ways of healing were determined to hold onto a mental concept, while their bodies were crying to be recognized and helped. Healing was increasingly becoming a personal path with no simple methods which would work for everyone.

Occasionally people came to us and said, "I'm sick, but I refuse to see a doctor. Will you help me?"

We were glad to help them, but usually only after they had seen a physician and had acknowledged some of their fears about their physical bodies. Many people needed to let go of their past hatred about previous experiences with doctors. Sometimes our work with them was about their relationship with medicine. Some people needed to see that God works through physicians as well as spiritual healers.

Other people came to us and said, "I've been visualizing my cancer cells being killed for months, but the cells keep multiplying. What am I doing wrong?"

For us, traditional treatments and visualizations often don't work, because they both include denial of the cause of the illness in the first place. Visualizing cancer cells killing each other can be just another expression of the body's conflict. So often, treatments and techniques are tried instead of risking and seeing what images and fears naturally surface to work with.

Sometimes we worked with people who had been seeing a therapist for months. All their tears and pain were on the surface, with no end in sight. As the therapist kept urging them to continue, we saw again that there was a denial, not of pain, but a denial of the existence of love and God within the person.

Whether we met people suffering from illness, destructive relationships, or financial crisis, in so many cases the energy which was blocked involved avoiding various parts of their humanness. The *Course* said:

> *"Health is the result of relinquishing all attempts to use the body lovelessly."[41] "It is not up to you to change your brother, but merely to accept him as he is. Any attempt you make to correct a brother means that you believe correction by you is possible and this can only be the arrogance of the ego."[42] "Think but an instant just on this, you can behold the holiness God gave His son and never need you think that there is something else for you to see."[43] "Spirit is in a state of grace forever. Your reality is only Spirit. Therefore you are in a state of grace forever."[44]*

Each session, each client risking to find a greater truth, carried us deeper into the meaning of the *Course*. We began to know that healing was so much more than the psychological theories, more even than the amount of spirit we had already opened to. We yearned to be with the psychic healers in the Philippines. We had heard from Greg and others about their ways of practicing seeing God in every part of their lives.

Beginning with the night long ago, when I saw the film about psychic surgery and heard the story of the businessman being healed, probably nothing else had shaken my psyche more profoundly. I wanted to know how matter could be manipulated so adroitly. I wanted to know more about this consciousness, the commitment of purpose to live in the spiritual world beyond the constant human temptations for security and comfort.

Within a few days of each other, both Genny and I had dreams of walking through foreign villages with people standing in lines for healing. In the dreams, we saw ourselves in primitive churches and felt the energy of the healers going down our spines and tingling in our fingers. On the physical plane, however, we had no idea how such a trip was going to happen.

Each month our income covered our living expenses, nothing more. *Hugs & Kisses* was in the stores and selling well. On Valentine's Day it was number eight on B. Dalton's Best Seller List. But we soon learned how many copies of the book would have to be sold before we would make any money. We would receive royalty checks only two times a year. The next check was not due until April.

The *Course* said:

". . . nothing is difficult that is wholly *desired."*[45]
"There are many answers you have received but have not yet heard."[46]

If we were to go to the Philippines, we would need more than our desire to bring it about. The place to start was the ranch where it all began. The man who had experienced the psychic surgery could give us the names of healers and tell us how to contact them. We were told to look for an English-speaking girl named Sophy Mendez and ask her to guide us. We spent an evening with people at the ranch, listening to stories and drawing maps which would lead us through various forks in the dirt roads and across bridges to huts in which healers could probably be found. The Philippine lowlands, where most of the healers live, is very rural and undeveloped.

There was so much to do and so many unknowns about our trip. How could we prepare for a trip that we couldn't afford right now? How could we best let Spirit translate our dreams and desires into physical form? We made a list of everything we would have to do to make such a trip. This included getting our passports validated again and finding someone to rent our home and office. Our goal was to have everything ready by the end of May. It was now the beginning of March.

The *Course* said:

> *"No one is where he is by accident and chance plays no part in God's plan."*[47] *"Be vigilant only for God and His Kingdom."*[48] *" 'Except you become as little children' means that unless you fully recognize your complete dependence on God, you cannot know the real power of the Son in his true relationship with the Father."*[49]

To depend upon the sales of *Hugs & Kisses* for our livelihood reminded us that just as we had depended upon love before, our future was constantly in hands greater than ours.

It is always such a delicate balance knowing when to take action and when to practice faith by waiting patiently. The only rule which seemed to work for us was not to act out of our need to do something to make it happen. Learning how much to do, how much to organize and plan, or how much to wait and see was quite a task.

The *Course* continued to speak to our egos:

> *"You must have noticed an outstanding characteristic of every end that the ego has accepted as*

*its own. When you have achieved it, it has not
satisfied you. That is why the ego is forced to shift
ceaselessly from one goal to another, so that you
will continue to hope it can yet offer you something."*[50]

We saw the part of ourselves which attempted to
make each day okay by hoping that something would be
different tomorrow. Was this the seductive dance of the
ego avoiding what is?

Both of us needed to take more time to meditate
and reaffirm our trust in the invisible. When we stopped
and took notice, we could see that the presence with us
was becoming as solid and as real as the chairs we were
sitting on. But unless we consciously chose to keep the
feeling with us, we would forget, and moments later we
would be chattering.

That spring we went through a ritual of consciously
asking God to come live with us. We pictured Him at the
table eating with us. At night we would offer Him our
bed. We asked ourselves, "If we had guests, would we be
as generous and honored to give to others as we were to
give to Him?" We invited Him on picnics and together
enjoyed looking over the hills to the ocean.

When we were happy, He was most happy. When we
were hurried, He stood there as if to say "Where are you
going?" When we were too busy talking to enjoy where we
were, He seemed not to notice. With incredible abandon-
ment he watched us yelling and screaming. He stood with
us as we watched a beautiful sunset or a garden in bloom.
He was so present, so real, that our times of unreality
were not experienced by Him. When we were denying our
peaceful centers, He was less apparent. We grew to notice
that it was not so much a question of how He was always
with us but how, so often, we were not with Him. All we
had to do was take the time to enjoy Him. But did we take
the time? Yes. And, so often, no!

If only we could live in a culture where He was
sought each day and was yearned for, above everything

else. We dreamed and imagined. Certainly that must be part of the secret of the healer, with whom God has achieved such an intimate relationship. So we waited for the circumstances of our lives to change to enable us to make the trip. Meanwhile, he filled our waiting with purpose, as if patience were also necessary and should have been on our list.

We took Him to meetings and into sessions with our clients. It was in the quiet moments, the moments between moments, that He was most giving to us. I remember one woman, in her sixties, who was constantly hearing voices. She had to use crutches because these voices were attacking her physically, entering her legs and back. Her doctors had only alienated her with their psychiatric labels pushing her further from normal life. She came to us because she realized that we would know she was not crazy but "psychic." How could Genny and I call her crazy when we, ourselves, have imaginary playmates! The major differences were that our visitors usually brought joy and that we could control the length of their visits. The challenge was not to convince this woman that her invisible visitors were not real but to support her in feeling that she was in control. We compared her mind to a radio antenna picking up frequencies which were too low and did not serve her. Like many of the people we have encountered who hear or see things, she strongly believed in God. So we decided that the only issue was to raise the frequency of her internal radio, so she would receive only peaceful messages. She agreed. Together we practiced meditating, especially when she felt she was under psychic attack. We repeated with her, "Only the peace of God is real, only God's perfect love is true." We did not want to struggle with the voices, to bring unnecessary attention to them, because that would only make them more real. We wanted to raise her frequency until she realized, as her doctors had told her, that they did not exist. In this approach, instead of feeling that she was wrong, she was finding something better to replace the destructive energy she believed was attacking her.

A man came to us who had a mass in his chest. The doctors thought it was cancer. He wanted to treat it holistically, instead of having radiation and chemotherapy to "blast it out" of him. Most of the holistic practitioners and healers he had seen told him what he had to change in order to get well. He had to change his diet, his feelings, his work, his relationships—seemingly everything. We could tell he was exhausted and burdened not only by the illness but by the thought of how much effort it would take for him to clean up his whole life. The stress of having so much to do was frightening him. We asked him to imagine the highest image of love. Together we went into the healing presence we had been feeling more and more. He saw a beautiful soft blue light. Together with that soft light, we surrendered to the love with us in that moment. He felt that peaceful light holding him, and for the first time in a very long time, he relaxed and felt loved. He knew he was going to be all right. That certainty of knowing came so sweetly and humbly that each of us could recognize the true source of the healing. We knew our work was to learn more and more about how to mobilize this force.

The following week someone called and wanted us to visit a man in his late twenties. He had been in a coma for over five months. He was about to get married, when he was involved in an accident. We walked into his hospital room and found a man who was hooked up to several awesome machines which were feeding him, breathing for him, and performing most of his normal bodily functions. Hardly any part of him seemed present. His fiancee's mother was with him. She had been there every single day since the accident. She had so badly wanted him as her son-in-law. Her daughter had accepted that he would probably die and had resumed a normal life. The rest of his family were dead. But this woman was telling us how determined she was that he live. She talked to him every day, and usually brought fresh flowers. We could see that she was his anchor here on earth. There was no one else. But was she willing to let him go if that's what he chose? We talked to her about accepting a higher destiny. She cried. No one else had ever questioned her role. To others, she was a heroine for being so giving. But to us, that giving felt so loaded with conditions that we were compelled to discuss it with her. When we did, she broke down. She admitted that she was using him. She was visiting the hospital every day, in hopes that he would live, because she didn't want to face what would happen to her and her family without him.

I looked at his body, controlled by the machines. I was turning green watching the lung machine inhale and exhale for him, forcing his chest to rise and collapse repeatedly. His face was expressionless, white. I was turning greener and greener. I was about to pass out, when Genny suddenly noticed and pulled me into the hall to get some air. "Remember," she said, "he is not his body."

She was right. I had been identifying with the form lying on the bed, instead of seeing him spiritually. I turned my mind to that image, and I saw him. He was caught between two worlds, afraid to come back and not quite willing to let go and go on. Together, Genny and I asked that his divine essence help him decide. As we meditated, we felt angels come into the room, and they held him. We knew that our goal was to love him right where he was, letting him decide whether to go on, to come back, or stay in between worlds—in a world of his own.

We went home. That evening the phone rang. A few hours after we left, he had made his decision. He had gone. It felt right, so right. His death truly was a victory that we all felt.

Another man had come to see us whose subsequent death also signaled a victory instead of a defeat. He was not very old but was obviously very ill. He came on the advice of his doctor who recognized the seriousness of his illness. A large part of his upper body had no feeling. It was like a dead weight. When he talked, he spoke of his illness as if part of his past was finally catching up with him and loading him down. We went into the middle of that weight during a laying on of hands, as he followed in a visualization exercise. We could feel so much light and gentleness just beneath the heaviness. He also reported seeing a light, like that of a candle, burning softly in the middle of the darkness.

A few days later we were told that he was in the hospital. Genny and I visited him and brought him a candle. We could see that he was very ill, and we felt it was important to remind him of what he saw during our time together. Three days after our visit, Genny awakened in the middle of the night. She had dreamed that the man had given back the candle saying, "I don't need it now." She felt very sure of the dream. We both meditated and felt a definite change in his condition. He felt so much lighter. We didn't know whether he had had a sudden recovery, or had died and connected with his own light.

The next morning when we called, we were not surprised that he had passed on in the night. Neither living nor dying feels like defeat. To us, it is the way we live and die that is either a success or a temporary loss of our greater being.

Clients with many different kinds of problems wove in and out of our lives. We never heard how things had finally turned out for many of them. Some people were instantly helped. Others felt that the weight was lightened but not completely gone. It was strange that although we would see such a variety of people, it felt like our work was the same with all of them. We were a little worried that we might be selecting a hammer to use on every problem because a hammer was the only tool we had. But no. Our purpose was to weave a golden thread through this material world we shared with others. And no matter what their current experience was, the purer our motivation, the more we felt connected to something beyond each of us. It was during these moments of weaving something very delicate, that Genny and I grew closer and our relationship became most alive.

The *Course* said:

*   *   *

"Nothing you undertake with certain purpose and high resolve and happy confidence, holding your brother's hand and keeping step to Heaven's song, is difficult to do."[51] *"Ultimately everyone must remember the Will of God, because ultimately everyone must recognize himself. This recognition is the recognition that his will and God's are one."*[52]

II

The Journey

Chapter Eight

✦ ✦

After twenty hours aboard a jet, we were in Hong Kong. We had a night's rest, and the next evening, we were landing in Bali, Indonesia. The last few weeks and days had easily led to the plane's waiting door. The royalty check for *Hugs & Kisses* arrived, giving us exactly the amount of money for our airfare and living expenses for the summer. When we returned, we would have to begin all over. But we were trying to live in the present more of the time instead of always being preoccupied with the future. For now, everything had come together, including seeing our last client two days before leaving.

On the way out the door, she had asked, "What else do you need for your trip?"

Genny and I looked at each other. "We're still looking for a camera," we said.

"Good," she said, "I have a brand new camera which needs a trip like yours to be broken in."

The lesson on the day we left read:

*   *   *

"When I said, 'I am with you always,' I meant it literally. I am not absent to anyone in any situation. Because I am always with you, you are the way, the truth, and the life."[53] *T. - 107*

The morning we awakened in Bali, it felt as if we had landed in a celestial dream greater than we had ever imagined. Our cottage sat in a sea of wild flowers. The sounds of the ocean called us from our bed. As we opened the door, we noticed a small bowl filled with rice and flowers on the step. The maid later told us that such a bowl would be placed there every morning to bless our awakening. As we walked about, we saw these offerings everywhere—in windows, next to trees, on car windshields, on the steps of buildings, and alone in the middle of a field. The Balinese are always making peace with nature spirits, with each other, with the spirits of loved ones who have passed on, with the God of love, and with the forces of temptation and evil. These peace offerings are given to the spirit in each thing or person, with the simple wish that the giver can feel at peace with this spirit.

We had decided to make this stop in Bali before going to the Philippines because Genny had been here once before, and she wanted me to feel its magic and experience the gentle simplicity of the people. The influence from the West had grown since her last visit, but not even the sounds of motorcycles and cars could eliminate the subtle feelings of grace inherent in the soul of the island.

The green tropical fields, the slow gait of the people carrying their wares, and the temples of all sizes in every conceivable place showed us that Bali had somehow escaped the effects of this century and perhaps even the last two or three. The people were not concerned with what normally occupies our western minds. They seemed shy and unusually reserved.

I was encouraged to rent a motorcycle in order to travel to the far side of the island which, we were told, remains much like Bali has always been. The only problem was that I had never driven a motorcycle before. After an hour's lesson, I was taken to City Hall to take a driving test that involved maneuvering the bike in and out of a long row of tires. I was given two chances. I failed each time. The boy from whom I was renting the bike spoke privately with the inspector, and it was announced that I could get a license anyway. For this friendly treatment, the fee was slightly more, of course.

In fact, the cost of the license almost included our lives. Chickens, dogs, and cows pulling carts did not give right-of-way to motorcycles on the road. Neither did the Balinese people who were driving trucks over one-lane bridges. When they saw a motorcycle coming from the other end, they proceeded as if the bridge were completely clear. Several times I was almost pushed into the river. On the roads the terror factor was high. In Bali everyone drove like the English—on the left side of the road.

The scenery, however, kept calling us down more and more small roads. Everywhere we saw rice fields, and people who were dressed in ceremonial outfits holding meetings and marching down small village streets. A holiday celebration was in progress in each town we visited. It seemed that almost every aspect of Balinese life was an occasion for ceremony and ritual. As we came around a bend into one small town, people were rushing through the streets carrying a coffin. They laughed and cheered as they tossed it, and carried it in and out of buildings and down alleys. They were followed by a crowd dancing and playing musical instruments.

"What are they doing?" we asked a young girl.

"They are busy confusing the spirit," she said. "When someone dies, we want to help the spirit go on, so we run with the body through the streets, hoping the spirit will become confused and not follow its former body. Then everyone celebrates, because we know the person has at last returned to his ancestors, and is home."

As we followed the crowd, we learned that there would be a fire ceremony that evening in the next town. We had heard about people walking on hot coals or glass while in a trance but had never thought we would actually witness it. As we entered this large grass hut, we saw several men building a pile of coconut shells at least three or four feet high, and setting them afire. An old man in a white robe appeared out of nowhere, walked right up to the intense flames, and sprinkled holy water on the growing fire. Then a young man appeared, wearing shorts. He was blessed with holy water as well. The man began to jump up and down on a straw horse. As the coals were spread out, the whole crowd was forced backwards because of the extreme heat. The old man in the white robe and the man on the horse spent a few more moments together. Suddenly the younger man began tossing himself into the air and dancing in the fire. The drumming had started as the dancer continued jumping into new piles of hot coals barefooted. There was nothing to prevent his straw horse from catching fire. As he spread the flames into a larger and larger circle, we kept moving back to protect ourselves from the heat and smoke. The dancer, meanwhile, was smiling. He rode his straw horse around and around. Suddenly, he stopped, still in the burning coals. Then just as suddenly, he would leap into the air again. We watched, amazed, as his straw horse went in and out of the flames, without a single strand catching fire. How could the dancer possibly bear the heat and flames? Finally, three men came out of the crowd and began circling the dancer. They wrestled him to the ground and pulled him away from the heat, as if he would not have stopped on his own. Then the man in the white robe appeared again, and blessed the dancer, who seemed to be awakening from a deep trance—from another world. We were told to come closer and look at his feet. There were no burns or blisters. How could he not have felt the heat? I could understand how the mind blocked the pain, but how did the body escape being burned by the fire, which at times shot several feet into the air?

The man in the white robe was the village shaman. In each village, specially selected people were trained to develop trance abilities. The shaman supervised the training. We watched him put two young girls into trance, and they performed a dance in celebration of the successful fire walk. The girls' movements were like those of butter-flies, rather than humans. They mirrored each other's gestures perfectly, and their bodies waved as if they were lighter than air. As I watched them move around the circle, I could almost hear them speaking to God. It was as if, through the movement of their bodies, they were saying, "I am one with You."

We were told that the gifted people of the village were mediums, expressing God through their particular creativity. It seemed that the purpose of the fire dance and of all their arts was to celebrate the existence of the supernatural. The ceremonies that we witnessed took their participants beyond their normal human potential. In one such dance, the participant would perform a special ritual to purify his heart of all guilt or temptation. When the purification ritual was completed, another dancer would try to stab him with a long silver sword. If his heart was pure enough, the sword would bend. All of Bali seemed to be in constant motion with dances and ceremonies that affirmed their living belief in a unique bond between the people, their ancestors, and God. I feel that the fire dance in Bali, like similar dances in other countries, must be a way of revealing God as a living, all powerful force.

After over a week of being confounded by the ways of this small island, we rested on Bali's quiet beaches on the far side of the island away from the larger towns. Children ran naked as they played with the balloons we had given them. We had a small hut to ourselves, where we slept without a sheet. Only the thatched roof was between us and the stars. Mealtime was a unique experience. The Balinese serve a meal as if waiting on royalty. The waiter would stand next to the table watching us eat, waiting to instantly serve our next request. The leftovers were thrown to scavenger dogs, which seemed to be everywhere. In Bali it is said that a thief will return as a dog in his next life. So as their own peculiar form of crime control, their dogs are half-starved and ignored. They are outcasts in the eyes of the Balinese. Even paradise has its own rules.

Before we left on our motorcycle tour of the island, we

had torn out pages from the *Course* to read in the next several days. We did not want to carry the heavy books on the bike. Then, as we finished each day's lesson, we gave them away to people we met. Each evening we watched the sunset. We had never felt heaven and earth so interconnected.

The words of the *Course* as usual fitted perfectly:

> *"Each day, each hour, every instant, I am choosing what I want to look upon, the sounds I want to hear, the witnesses to what I want to be the truth for me."*[54] W. - 422

We passed the lesson along to the sweet innkeeper who could not do enough to make us feel comfortable. He accepted the lesson as a gift, as a special prayer. We thanked him for his friendship.

We had only a few days left before our planned departure from the island. On the way back to our home base on the main part of the island, we found that the road had almost been washed out by rain. There always seemed to be a large truck behind every blind turn. At one point, we came to a turn, and there simply wasn't enough room for both the truck coming towards us and our cycle. I turned sharply in an attempt to get off the road. The cycle's wheels spun in the mud and slid out from under us. We were tossed alongside the road. Slowly we picked ourselves up and finished the trip. We couldn't wait to return the cycle and be on our own two feet again.

Late that evening, we finally arrived back at our home base. For the next two days, we did nothing else but sleep and take walks. One morning the maid came to the hut. She told us her name was Komang. Her face was all swollen, with her jaw and cheeks expanded to twice their normal size.

"What's wrong?" we asked.

"Lower spirits," she replied.

"Can we help?" Genny asked.

We explained to her that we did natural healing. Komang immediately became quite interested when we described our healing work. Genny asked her to sit on the bed. Then she gently placed her hands on the girl's face. She seemed to melt with the energy. Genny had her lie down, and she became very quiet and beautifully at ease.

That evening she came to find us. The swelling was completely gone. "What did you do?" she asked Genny.

We explained that the "lower spirits," which caused the ailment, could be healed with "higher spirits," or love. Komang intuitively and immediately understood what we meant. She told us that Balinese medicine men and women use herbs and rituals to take off the hex of jealousy, anger, and the darkness of vengeful spirits. As we discussed more about her ailment, she became excited. With a shy intensity, Komang invited us to visit her family.

Their small house was in a village not too far from the main town on the island. When we entered, we were welcomed instantly by the entire family. After a short time, Komang asked Genny if we would go to the village where her brother lived and work on him.

We left immediately. Within a half-hour, we were being led through a small alleyway to the house of Komang's brother. We were taken into a little room where a young man was lying on a grass bed. He appeared to have a fever. Genny worked with him for about ten minutes. By the time she was done, a half-dozen people had gathered outside, watching, and waiting for their turn to be healed. Laying-on-of-hands was new to them, but only as a form of healing. The healing itself was instantly accepted. We had never met people who were so receptive, so naturally believing. It was as if they started feeling the energy and soaking it up even before they were touched. One at a time, they came inside and lay on the grass bed. They were so sensitive to the subtle flow of the healings that Genny worked with each person for only a few minutes. Their faces said so much. We bowed to each other in gestures of mutual thanks, and then departed.

The following morning we were to leave for the next part of our journey. We were going first to Singapore, then Bangkok, and finally to the Philippines.

Our last night in Bali was spent sitting on the beach, quietly talking, remembering, and meditating. A family, dressed in ceremonial costumes, came towards us. They were playing drums and horns. One member of the group slowly carried a large bowl of ashes, which she emptied into the ocean. A young girl standing next to us explained that the ashes of a loved one were being returned to the Infinite. The family stood around chanting to their ancestors. They sang words of peace and gratitude for receiving the spirit. It was a farewell that we had never experienced before. As we watched, we could see and feel that there was only joy for the one who had now been released to true freedom.

We found Singapore to be a jet-age city, in the middle of a part of the world where oxen and grass huts were still the primary way of life. After experiencing Bali, with its silent offerings reflecting a oneness with nature, we were back in a clean, efficient, and noisy city. After only a day, when we were sitting in a cafe, I had a headache and began feeling feverish. I guessed that my body was adjusting to the different climate and culture. We went to a beautiful park called the Chinese Gardens, hoping to find a place to rest and recuperate before I really became sick.

Once there, I immediately had to lie down. We spotted a large old tree whose branches were touching the sky and also bent to the ground. There was a pond and waterfall next to it. I asked the ground for permission to sit on it and be nurtured. I was welcomed. Genny talked to the tree and was told to take a certain part of its roots, which were sticking out of the ground, and put them on me. She did this, and then took some mud from the bottom of the pond and rubbed it on my forehead. Afterwards she blessed me with some water. I felt better. It was getting late. But we still had a long bus ride back to the city and our hotel. Just as we were thinking that there were too few cars around to find a ride, a small white car appeared from out of nowhere, and the driver asked us if we wanted a lift. Since he spoke English, we struck up a conversation and friendship with him in no time. He was eager to give us a ride all the way to our hotel, despite it being some way off his normal route home.

Late that night, the fever came back. For the next forty-eight hours, I shivered and sweated as my temperature climbed above 102 degrees. We finally agreed it was time to find a doctor to find out what was wrong. We had tried everything we knew to do. But now, being ill in a foreign country, where we knew no one, was beginning to frighten us. We were sorry we hadn't gotten the name of the man who had picked us up a few days before. The hotel clerk told us about a modern clinic down the street. After a brief check-up, the doctor gave me antibiotics, explaining that if they didn't help, I should get a blood test in the next few days, because my symptoms were those of malaria.

By the next evening, it was apparent that the drugs had been useless. Now I was having hallucinations, caused by the high fever. Everything seemed disoriented. We had planned to go to Bangkok, but considering my situation, we decided to fly directly to Manila. We had been told about a team of psychic surgeons working in a downtown hotel there.

It turned out that the hotel was just across the street from the American Embassy, one block away from the Hilton. We tried to imagine psychic healers working in a modern, deluxe hotel in the middle of a downtown area in an American city. It was a normal occurrence for groups of foreign tourists to fly in to see the healers, and stay at the hotel. We weren't part of such an organized tour, but the office manager agreed I could see the healers in the morning.

All night I ached, feeling pain and weakness in every part of my body. I slept fitfully. I dreamed that there was a white cloth lying next to my face. I tried to see the image of God or an angel in that sheet—or something, anything! But there was nothing. Then I felt my body being dressed, calmed, and prepared, as if for surgery. I woke up knowing that today, finally, I was going to get well.

After sitting in a waiting room that morning, we were escorted into a small plain room with only a table in the middle. The psychic surgeon and several of his assistants welcomed us. I explained I was feeling very ill because of the constant fever. With nothing else said, he asked me to lie down on my stomach. Genny was allowed to stay and take pictures. He started to work on the base of my neck. How did he know that this was exactly where I had felt so much tension after our motorcycle adventure in Bali? It was only after he started kneading the area around my shoulders that I made the connection of this pain to my fear of being seriously hurt in Bali. I found myself deeply relaxing. It felt as if my lower neck were being massaged.

Suddenly I felt energy pour over me as if I were in a shower of light. The surgeon told me to turn my head so I could see the lump of flesh he had taken out of my upper back. He calmly washed his hands as I just lay there. It was all so quick, the entire procedure lasted no more than two minutes. I stood up, a bit shaky on my feet, and instantly noticed that my fever was gone.

Then Genny lay down. She pointed to where she had been having occasional stomach pains for many months. The healer instantly put his hands on the spot. As his fingers touched the skin, it parted, and blood began oozing out of the hole. He put his finger deeper inside of her stomach, and lifted out a piece of tissue. Genny seemed very calm, in spite of having an open wound. As the surgeon removed his fingers, the hole in her skin began to close. There was no scar, not even a mark, where she had moments before been cut open. The assistant wiped the blood away from the smooth white skin of Genny's abdomen. During the entire procedure I had been taking pictures, standing no more than two feet away. What I had just seen made no sense to me, yet somehow felt very natural. It was as if some impurity was simply lifted out of Genny's stomach. She stood up, feeling very peaceful and happy.

The next day we went to see another healer who lived in Manila named Alex. He did laying-on-of-hands with me, as I was having difficulty adjusting to the intense heat and humidity. Genny's stomach was still sore, so he performed additional psychic surgery on her. He was casually dressed and very matter-of-fact about the whole procedure. As had happened before, he let his fingers lay on Genny's belly, and without any sharp instrument or anesthesia, he dug his hand further through the skin and into the organs beneath. While standing there, with his fingers entirely inside of Genny, he said, "My hands are instruments for spirit doctors."

For a good thirty seconds, I stood there watching his hand piercing deeper and deeper into Genny's stomach until it was half way inside her. He finally pulled his hand out. In it was a piece of fatty tissue. He wiped the blood off her stomach, which appeared slightly red, but otherwise normal.

For the next three days, Genny lay in bed, unable to get around. She felt as if she had been through a major operation. We went back to see Alex for an explanation. He told us, "Psychic surgery is an old ritual which has come down from the mountains just in the last forty years. Before then, its secret was known only to the medicine man who passed it on to his apprentices, generation after generation. For a long time only one man performed the openings. Then during the Second World War, when there was very little medicine and no doctors available to the people, a healer named Papa Terte, trained several more healers. Since then, the Espiritistas, as we are called, have grown. We are located all over the Philippines, but most of us are living on the main island of Luzon."

"But what about the openings?" I asked, needing more facts. "How does the surgery work?"

He sat for a minute, staring at us. Then, as if speaking from a distance, he said, "You will understand more fully one day. For now, let me explain it this way." His attention still seemed to be split. "In our three dimensional world, this table is solid, and, of course, I cannot put my hand through it. But there's another level of consciousness, a fourth dimension, where this table becomes like liquid, and, of course, I can put my hand into it and then pull it out. Then the table returns to normal. In the operations, the healer sees the body as a bowl of water. So he puts his hand in and pulls out the impurity creating the illness. When he takes his hand out, the body heals instantly, just as water would return to its normal state. But you must remember, the healer does not do the healing. His hands are only instruments of a higher energy."

As impressed as we were with the story, we were equally impressed by his perfect English. He told us that he had been born to very poor parents, and had never gone to school. When he was fourteen, his skill in speaking English came in a strange way. Night after night he had had intense dreams. After that, he began to speak English spontaneously. The story was hard to believe. But the events of the last few days were equally hard to rationalize. We decided that there was no reason to doubt his story or make judgments one way or another.

On Sunday, we drove out to the countryside with Alex. After driving for hours on a major road from Manila and then several miles along dirt roads, we pulled up to a small concrete building next to a rice field. We went inside. This was the poor church where Alex had grown up.

The service had already started, and it continued on for several hours more. Genny and I just sat there, looking around, not understanding any of the language being used. The Espiritista Church did not look like the Catholic Churches we'd seen elsewhere in the Philippines and in other third world countries. There were no crosses or artifacts on the walls. Hanging on the front wall were cloth pennants imprinted with the name of the church and passages from the Bible.

The heat of the day continued to grow more intense. We tried meditating, thinking of something other than being uncomfortable, and doubting our purpose for being there. As the sun was setting, people began to leave. Alex had disappeared. Now there was no one with us who spoke English except one toothless old man. He summoned us and then asked us to follow him. Without ques-

tioning what was happening, we did so. We dragged our
baggage behind us, as we followed him about a mile down
another small road.

He stopped in front of a small and dusty concrete
shelter, and then led us upstairs to a little room with a
mattress on the floor. He smiled saying, "My home is your
home."

We thanked him. As we looked around, the bare
mattress on the floor seemed very inviting. Later, we
awakened to find him beside us, holding out a bowl of rice
for dinner with some unidentifiable vegetable on the side.
As it grew darker, we realized that he had no electricity or
plumbing. He had only a small lantern for all of us to
share. We finished the simple meal, and he took the bowls
from us.

We told him that we wanted to study with the
healers. He nodded, then left the room. Soon he returned
with a Bible. We reminded him that we hoped to meet the
healers. He continued nodding. "Read this," he said, "just
read this." We were tired and confused. We hadn't come
several thousand miles just to read the Bible.

The room was full of mosquitos, because there was
no glass in the windows panes. It was late, and still very
hot and humid. Genny was feeling weak, as she was still
adjusting to the climate. We looked at each other and
didn't know whether to cry or laugh. "What are we doing
here?" we said to each other simultaneously. We couldn't
imagine how we were going to spend the next several
months. With the bugs and the heat, we weren't even sure
how we would get through the night!

The next morning the old man cheerfully brought
us more white rice. Pointing to the Bible, he said, "Did
you have a good night?"

We assured him that we did, and we began packing
our things. We didn't know where we were going, but we
knew this was not our final destination. The old man
urged us to stay. But we thanked him, picked up our
baggage and walked out onto the dirt road. We stood
there wondering which way to go. We had no idea where

we were. I had lost the names and addresses we had gotten at the ranch, remembering only the name of the girl we were to look up and the town she lived in.

We noticed several small busses passing in both directions. Without any other choice, we stepped on one of these small buses, hoping that it would take us to a town. The bus was filled with people carrying many things—produce from the market, chickens, dogs, babies, and packages. We squeezed into a seat near the back. As the bus started, I turned to a woman behind us and asked if she had ever heard of a person named Sophy Mendez from a town called Binalonan. I was hoping to find out if we were at least going in the right direction. The woman just stared at me, shaking her head.

At that moment, a young girl in front of me said in English, "Who are you looking for?"

I repeated the name, "Sophy Mendez."

"That's me," she said.

We got off the bus two stops later. Sophy was full of energy, and eager to help us. Best of all, she understood what we were looking for, and she knew all the local healers. That afternoon we set out to meet some of them. They all worked in their own primitive churches spread out through the countryside.

"The most famous healer," she said, "is Josephina Sison. She has tours of foreigners coming to see her every day. It's quite a trip to her place, but let's try it."

After many miles of dirt roads leading us deeper and deeper into the countryside, we arrived at a small cluster of simple houses and a little chapel. A tour bus had just arrived, and the Japanese tourists were getting off. We went inside the church and walked up front to see what was going on.

Josephina was standing behind a table on which a little boy was lying. She took a wad of cotton and poured oil on it. The boy was obviously crippled and appeared nervous. Then Josephina held the cotton up to the flag hanging overhead and seemed to be blessing it. We had manuevered our way to be within inches of her. She began to push the cotton into the boy's deformed arm. I stood there, watching her push the last bit of the cotton effortlessly into the skin until it disappeared. She looked directly at me, then in a calm, friendly manner said, "This is to absorb impurities in the body." She moved to the boy's shoulder, and began to slowly withdraw cotton through the skin. The boy's arm began to shudder, and as we watched, it straightened. She told the parents to bring the boy back tomorrow. Genny and I looked at each other and had to sit down. The energy I could feel all around the table was affecting our equilibrium, physically as well as mentally.

We sat there in disbelief. Moments before we had been standing on each side of the table. Any sleight of hand by the woman could not have gone undetected. Yet, to understand what we had just seen as sleight of hand was the only way our minds could cope with it. But how could a deception have straightened out the obviously withered arm of the boy? The boy had been healed. I looked at Josephina, whose face was as smooth and as loving as that of Jesus in the picture next to her on the wall. I wondered how she could be healing people if this were only an illusion?

Looking around, we could see no evidence that she was healing all these people just for the money. Her surroundings were primitive. These people wouldn't have come all this way unless she had a reputation for helping others.

We watched her work on a few more people. With each person she repeated the same ritual of taking the cotton, blessing it, putting it in one part of the body, and taking it out somewhere else. When we watched, allowing ourselves to simply feel the energy of the situation, it all felt natural, although I couldn't begin to explain why. When our minds tried to intervene and figure out exactly what was occurring, we felt nauseated. The world of our rational mind and the world of this simple, plain peasant woman could not be mixed. We were dimensions apart. No amount of physical maneuvering to bring us closer or to see from a different angle would change what we were seeing. We either had to enter her subjective awareness or move further from the table. If we stood next to the table and tried to evaluate what we saw, we became dizzy and disoriented again. We watched her working on twenty or thirty people, each one for only a minute or two, before we felt weak and tired. The room felt so alive and full of light, but our minds were exhausted from their persistent efforts to understand or explain. We left the chapel, moving in a very tenuous reality.

Sophy took us to a small motel in a nearby town for the night. She would come for us early in the morning. We were so tired that we couldn't even react to the three-inch long insects crawling on the floor and flying across the dark room.

The next morning Sophy hurried us to our first stop. She had told us that one healer did his healing work only in the early hours of the day, before going to work in the fields. In front of his small chapel, which was bordered by a large field, we were told to leave our camera outside. Sophy explained that very few foreigners visited here and that the healer did not like cameras interfering with the service. The church was full. We took seats which were off to one side. This church looked like the others we had seen, a simple concrete structure with flags on the wall.

We had twenty minutes to read and meditate. We could not understand the service, so we began to read our lessons from the *Course,* which we had grabbed on our way out the door that morning.

> *"What could you not accept, if you but knew that everything that happens, all events, past, present, and to come are gently planned by One whose only purpose is your good?"*[55] W.-247

At the end of the brief service, the healer pointed to a woman and motioned for her to come up front. She lay down on a plain wooden table and adjusted her clothing to expose her stomach. The healer picked up a large silver spoon, placed it on her stomach, and began to push it into her belly. The woman instantly cried out as she felt the spoon piercing her skin. The healer paid no attention. He began shoving the spoon in and out of her stomach, pulling out bits and pieces of tissue. There was blood everywhere. Finally he removed the spoon. Someone came up to hold and comfort the woman. She gradually quieted down.

The healer proceeded to point to other people in the audience and repeated the same operation on different parts of their bodies. All I could think was that I hoped his finger wouldn't turn in my direction.

He called up a man who had a swollen jaw, probably from an infected tooth. The healer put his hand under the flag on the wall and seemed to be asking for something. Then he turned back to the patient, put two fingers into his mouth and made a fantastic jerk, pulling the tooth out in the same moment. Everyone was very pleased except the man with his mouth open. He was in lots of pain. Finally he got up and showed everyone the space in his mouth where the tooth was. Sophy translated, telling us that the tooth was never loose but had been very infected and sore for weeks.

Sophy explained that each healer has different gifts and methods. We always thought a spiritual surgeon ought to do his work painlessly. My friend Alberto had told us about primitive healers in Mexico and Brazil who would use a knife, without administering an anesthetic, creating little or sometimes lots of pain. But hearing stories was one thing and personally seeing someone stick a large spoon into a person's body and seemingly scoop out raw tissue was another. All we could do was try to refrain from analyzing the experience from our rational perspective.

It was now early afternoon. Both Genny and I had become impatient to find someone with whom we could feel some connection. The healers so far were fascinating but had no interest in our visit. We were just visitors in this time and space. There had to be something more.

We ate a quick meal of fruit bought in an open market. Then we followed Sophy to the home of another healer. This man, known as an international medium, had traveled to Europe and often had foreigners living with him. After changing several buses along dusty roads in the overwhelming heat, we arrived. His home was deserted. A field worker nearby volunteered his conjecture that the healer was away, traveling in the mountains. We had been told that the healers often did missionary work, helping the very poor who lived in remote areas. He could be gone a week, or a month, or longer. We were disappointed.

The bus ride back to our hotel was again full of people, and we were squished together between two workers who were smelling of sweat and field dirt.

Sophy turned and said, "I don't know why, but I think I should take you to see a woman I know. She does not do the physical openings, but she is an excellent medium. She has many gifts, including laying-on-of-hands. Her name is Paz."

We got off the bus and walked the short distance to Paz's home. She greeted us from a chair, and asked us to sit down next to her. With no preamble, she immediately went into trance. The voice of the guide speaking through her said, "This medium is here to serve you. She has been expecting you. You will spend the summer here. If your heart remains pure, this medium will give you all of her spiritual gifts before you return home."

Genny and I were dumbfounded, yet not completely so. After all, we had asked for exactly what Paz had just extended to us. She came out of trance and someone else in the room told her what she had just said, because she does not remember what occurs while she is in trance. Paz listened, then jumped up and said to both of us very excitedly, "Welcome, welcome. I have a room for you upstairs." Paz hugged us again, obviously full of joy. "A very special medium who lives high in the mountains prophesied your trip and told me you would be coming."

Chapter Nine

Everything was happening so fast. After having had no real connection with the people we were meeting, here we were with Paz—expected guests. We immediately decided to stay for dinner, return to our hotel for the night, and move into Paz's home the next morning. Everything felt right.

That evening the grandmother of the family was brought from next door to meet us. She was very old. As she watched, waiting, Paz proceeded to give us some pass words "to increase the magnetism in our hands." Then we were asked to pray for the grandmother and do laying-on-of-hands. We did not know exactly what was wrong with the grandmother, but it didn't matter. Everyone knew it was a special day. Prophecy had come true. Spirit had successfully guided us all together. A strong presence of the Divine could be felt in the house. We simply shared the fullness of our thanksgiving for the day's events as Paz and her family stood by and watched. Everyone knew it wasn't our energy which was being directed to the grandmother, but that we were using our filled hearts as the source of our prayers for complete healing.

Much later we returned to the hotel. We turned on the light and watched several giant cockroaches scramble across the room. We realized we were too excited to care. During the night, however, as we heard their scraping movements, we became more impatient and were so glad we were leaving in the morning.

I dreamed I was walking down the village street holding Genny's hand. Then I was told not to think in terms of "I" anymore. Neither was I to think in terms of Genny and me. I understood that from now on I must think only in terms of We: the Holy Spirit, Genny, and myself—for nothing ever separates us.

Looking through the *Course* before breakfast the next morning, one paragraph suddenly appeared to reach out to us:

> *"You will undertake a journey because you are not at home in this world. And you will search for your home whether you realize where it is or not. If you believe it is outside you the search will be futile, for you will be seeking it where it is not."*[56]
> *T. -209*

As we carried our baggage into Paz's home, she had just finished emptying her room, moving her clothes downstairs into the room where her sister slept. "You will have my room," she told us.

That evening we learned that in giving us her bed, she would be sleeping on the floor of her sister's room with two other women. We lay awake remembering that Alberto had once told us that it is an honor to sleep in a healer's bed. In fact, it is said that many people have been healed of all kinds of ailments simply from resting in a place used every night by a healer.

Paz gave us two Psalms to read each night and morning. She told us that Psalms 51 and 63 are part of most mediums' training. The Bible was a source from which it had not been easy for us to receive. We had difficulty reading about all the violence, even in the lyrical Psalms, where after only a few expressions of sweet softness, liars and thieves are being doomed forever. But as we read we decided that maybe our discomfort with the violence came from our inability to look at it in the world and in ourselves as well. What parts of us are also liars and thieves on some level of our being? What part of us just takes from the world as if it is ours to take? How naked in our honesty are we really?

That first night Genny and I lay in bed talking, while outside the family's large dog barked angrily. The dog was in no sense a pet, but a guard, a trained killer chained near the rice storage bin. All night he stood guard. We thought, "This must be part of the violence we didn't want to accept." We lay there, trying to send love to the dog and wanting him to feel it, to be calmed, to sleep, so that we might also sleep. I remembered the passage in the *Course* that says:

> "*. . . exempt no-one from your love, or you will be hiding a dark place in your mind where the Holy Spirit is not welcome. And thus you will exempt yourself from his healing power, for by not offering total love you will not be healed completely.*"[57]
> T. - 227

I felt my temper rising. Beside me, Genny was also beginning to stiffen resentfully. Last night the cockroaches, tonight this mad dog. Is this some kind of test for us? At last, as dawn approached, I was able to sleep—very briefly. Light coming through our window awakened us. We took down the bug-netting which had been stretched over the bed, and then we dressed. Awaiting us downstairs was a large bucket of water for us to wash with. The toilet, like others we had encountered, had no seat. We tried squatting instead. Paz's home had electricity, but no plumbing. All cooking was done outside in an open pit.

Breakfast was waiting for us, fish and white rice, the same breakfast we would be served throughout our stay. Paz insisted we eat first while the rest of the family stood around doing chores or watching. That, too, would be the pattern for all our meals.

It wasn't until that morning that we realized how many people lived in this one house. Paz, her two sisters, one sister's husband, two children, and a woman who helped care for the family made up the household. The grandmother lived next door with more relatives. There were so many people in such close proximity, yet we never once heard anyone fighting or any children screaming.

That morning, as always, when a child came into the room, he or she would approach the oldest person in the room, take that person's hand, and put it to the child's forehead, as a sign of respect. A quiet home was natural for them.

We spent the day quietly relaxing around the house. After a nap in the afternoon and more meditation, Paz called us into the yard. "Did you see the visitor today?" she asked.

We shook our heads. "No," we answered.

"Did you feel him?" she continued. We weren't certain. "Well, an angel was present in the house all day." She pointed to one room where he had been, and we could now sense the lightness of some presence. "It's a good sign. It means your visit is blessed."

Paz went into the living room, sat down, picked up her Bible, and as quickly and effortlessly as taking a breath, went into trance. A spirit voice, unlike that of her normal voice, came through Paz and identified himself as Paul from the New Testament. "This medium is to train you and pass along all her gifts. Before you return home, you will have in one summer what has taken her twenty years to learn. Pray to feel worthy. There is great need of your service. Many are praying for your development so many can be helped. Do not worship false idols, for by doing so you are limiting God."

Paz came out of trance. "False idols? What does that mean?" Genny asked Paz. Paz told us to meditate and pray. We left the house to take a long walk up and down the small streets of the town. I felt guilty because I knew money must be my false idol. I had spent so much time budgeting, planning, and scheming about our funds for the summer. How could I let go and trust in one moment of surrender and then, minutes later, hold onto every dollar as if it were the last?

Genny discussed her "false idols"—her need for sleep and material comfort. She would say, "I'll follow God as long as I have something clean to wear and a full night's sleep."

Up one street and down another we unmasked our idols, our Western selfishness. Our attachments seemed so strong. How could we be worthy of God when our personalities were so determined to stand in the way? Despite all the work we had done, our egos felt bigger than ever.

Much later on, still heavily weighted down by our doubts, we returned to the house and asked Paz to tell us her story. How did she overcome her personal desires and give herself so completely to spirit?

"I resisted my mediumship three times," Paz replied. "When I was a young woman, I was told by three different mediums that I would become a medium and a healer. Each time I refused. I did not believe in the Espiritista way. My family always expected me to be a teacher, and I wanted to teach, like my sisters had. Why were these mediums telling me this? I didn't want to do what they said. One morning, several months after my last reading, I awakened very, very ill. I could not get out of bed. For many days I suffered severe pains. The doctors had nothing to help me, so I became very frightened. Then I remembered the medium's readings. At that instant, I saw an angel coming to me in a great white light. I knew I was being given a choice to serve or go on and die. Would I give myself for higher service? Reluctantly, I agreed. I began training with a local medium. My family was very unhappy about this. They resisted for years and fought with me. I knew I could not change their minds. I would go to my room, crying and praying for healing. Over the years I offered no resistance to my family but prayed instead, prayed for their hearts to soften. After many, many years, my new life was accepted by them, and each one in my family gradually accepted Espiritism ... except one." Paz pointed to one sister who still, eighteen years later, did not believe. Paz smiled. "She too will someday accept God."

Genny and I reflected on her story. We couldn't imagine living under the same roof with one's family and offering no resistance. We tried to picture ourselves with the strength to listen to and honor our own inner voices and guidance. Would we have the same will to live our path in spite of our family's resistance and cultural disbelief? Above all, what amazed me about Paz's story was her reluctance to serve and her being practically chased by Spirit until she accepted her destiny. How many other stories had we heard about healers who finally succumbed when a dream or psychic reading told them of their higher path? What about us? We had not been chased. If anything, we were chasing God, asking for gifts. Maybe we were being too arrogant.

That night we were taken to meet Eduardo, another medium. On our way to the service, we heard his story. For most of his life he had been a cock-fighter. One day when he was in the fields with his ox, he had an accident. At that moment, he saw God appear to him, telling him not to fight cocks anymore. Since then he had given his life to service and opened his barn to any neighbors who wished to come on Thursday evenings. He is called Old Man Eduardo because he is well into his eighties.

As we walked in, I was taken by this simple old man. He was dressed in overalls and stood humbly in front of a group of people seated on benches. Eduardo was very pleased to see us and acted as if our coming were a sign for him and his family. He looked at us with eyes that saw so much. From his reaction, I sensed that our presence was a metaphor of some kind for his own spiritual journey. In a dimly lit room, everyone was quiet. He entered trance quickly. As I was watching, everyone paid close attention to each spoken word. "Everything that happens in one's life has special meaning," he said. "Everyone's presence can be used to seek something greater, to understand spirit in a deeper way."

One by one people stepped to the front. Eduardo blessed them. Then we were called, and someone stood next to us to help with the translation. We were told to open our hands and receive a gift. The old man held the Bible over our open hands. I closed my eyes. I felt pressure against both my hands, as if something were indeed being given to me. I opened my eyes to check. My hands were empty. I closed my eyes again. I saw in my mind's eye that my hands were filled with white grain. As I was about to tell what I saw, Genny said, "I see white flour or grain in my hands."

The old man said, "You are receiving spiritual nourishment to strengthen you. You must not worship false idols. You must not limit God."

"Oh, no. Not again, the same warning," I was thinking. I felt myself close to falling into inescapable despair.

Old Man Eduardo continued, "When you meditate, you have pictures of God which you meditate on. Those pictures are idols and limit God. Let the pictures come to you freely. Let them go freely. Do not hold onto yesterday in your meditations today. Do not limit God by holding onto those limited visions and experiences."

Suddenly I felt lifted. I no longer felt doomed by the weights of my personality. I realized at that moment that God does not even see this part of me. What is perfect sees only the part of me which is also whole. God sees only Himself in each of us and says, "Do not limit who I am." It all made sense. If we are learning not to judge others, I must learn not to judge myself, including even those weaknesses I don't like. If we are to learn to see God in others, we must know that truly God is without judgment and sees only Himself in us.

The next morning Genny and I read from the *Course* as we lay in bed:

> "Do not accept this little fenced off aspect as yourself. The sun and ocean are as nothing beside

what you are. The sunbeam sparkles only in the sunlight, and the ripple dances as it rests upon the ocean. Yet in neither sun nor ocean is the power that rests in you." "The thought of God surrounds your little kingdom, waiting at the barrier you built to come inside and shine upon the barren ground. See how life springs up everywhere."[58] T.-265

That day Paz again instructed us to meditate and read the Psalms. Each day the poetry was easing deeper within both of us. The flavor of each word was like a fulfilling grain of spiritual nourishment. Paz said, "Read this morning, and this afternoon I will take you to our church and you will bathe. The waters are blessed and will help purify you for your upliftment."

We returned to our room, and went back and forth from the Bible to the *Course*, which often spoke closest to us:

"As faithlessness will keep your little kingdoms barren and separate, so will faith help the Holy Spirit prepare the ground for the most holy garden that He would make of it."[59] T. 824

At the church we were taken to the back of the concrete block building. A large bowl of very cold water from the well was brought to us. We took off our clothes and quickly poured the water over us and welcomed the hot sun warming us again. Paz told us to sit in the church, pray, and try to see the spirits which stand up front. Feeling a soft peacefulness, we looked at the banners hanging on the walls, but neither of us saw anything specific. The bath had deeply refreshed us but we couldn't pinpoint any special awareness. "Be patient," said Paz. "Be patient."

The next morning we were taken to another holy well for a cleansing ritual similar to the one of the previous day. Close beside this small hut in the countryside, several people were lying around. Their limbs were deformed. Paz said that many people had been healed here. Genny and I discussed the story in the Bible that tells of Jesus coming to a well where the crippled attempt to get into the water each time the angel approaches the pool. Here, the crippled were also waiting for a sign—hoping for a miracle. There was one man with a grotesque goiter, the size of a large grapefruit, distorting his face and throat. He seemed to be in so much pain. It was so hard to remember that when we empathize, we must not join in another's suffering. We prayed at the well for him. A strange impulse stopped me before I began to pray. I felt that I must first acknowledge the part of myself which is grotesque and unsightly. We prayed for God's forgiveness and healing.

Paz told us to stand looking into the well. Both of us saw a tunnel of light leading into the water. First Genny, and then I, drank the water. It tasted absolutely terrible. But we prayed for cleansing. Paz slipped into trance, and Spirit spoke again. "A medium becomes blessed when he is worthy in God's sight. Only forgiveness and cleansing can prepare you. Many foreigners come here to the Philippines and boast of their strict diets, yoga, and long fasts. But the only fast God sees is a fast of prayer. He does not care about what you eat or how much you suffer for Him. He wants only his children to be pure and of clean heart."

I asked, "What do you mean, fast on prayer?"

Paz, still in trance, answered, "Tonight you will begin. For seven days you will pray every three hours around the clock. Some of the great mediums in the Philippines sometimes fast on prayer for seventy-two days."

That night we prepared to begin our fast. We would eat normally, but every three hours we would meditate and read the Psalms. Before everyone went to sleep, Paz again went into trance and performed healings on people who came to see her. We were asked to help.

The week was spent continuing our prayer fast. As the days went by, we began noticing the difference between the energies and spirits we were experiencing. It was becoming clearer to us that energy is not simply energy. The Shamanic path given to us by Doris, and the healing energy tapped by the Philippine healers, had important differences.

Doris wanted us to see the spirit in everything. For her the spirit was the living force, or the aura, in trees, humans, flowers—in all of nature. That force could tell us the complete history of what we were looking at, and all of its needs. Doris wanted us to become allies with nature to enable us to call upon its strength. The Shaman acknowledges the perfect order in nature and then breathes underwater, finding life even in death, while walking a path above the earth. Spirits of friends, loved ones, and even animals are communicated with, giving signs for us to follow. The energy Doris revealed to us was familiar, of the earth, strong and directional.

Personal power was what had importance, and personal power came about by living purposefully, by being awake and always listening to the world communicating to itself. Personal power and responsibility were the same thing. In Doris' world, there are no accidents. There are no excuses, no blaming our problems on others. The reason for the world being in the shape it's in is that many people want the world to care for them without assuming any responsibility for their own relationship to the earth. Being able to give to the earth as much as we take from it is what is going to realign us with nature.

In Paz's view, the person is nothing. The word "power" is foreign to her awareness. Only by having complete humility, almost to the point of absolute denial of self, may one then become ready and worthy to feel God's love. Here, the presence we felt was celestial and peaceful, as if it were leading us beyond ourselves and beyond the earth's vibration. Doris used herbs and nature spirits to heal. Paz was seeking to be God's instrument, attempting to demonstrate God's existence as the source of our healing.

The Shaman addresses the aura of the person, including that of each organ, each life cycle of the spirit, and those aspects of nature in close proximity to the patient. The Philippine healers talked of heaven and going home. Slowly I was realizing that there are many kinds of energy. The spiritual world is vast and complex beyond easy conclusions and assumptions. As Westerners, we open up to energy not knowing what we are opening up to or why. Psychic impressions enter our minds, and we think these phenomena are something special. I was beginning to suspect that it is only after committed discipline that our hearts will restore our vision of God.

Our days had become so emptied of activities that we found ourselves sorting out our lives and becoming clearer as to what had led us here. I began to see how I had needed to explore my own feelings and accept my emotional extremes. I could see how arrogant I was in thinking that I now knew something about the true nature of our being. I had needed Doris to deflate my limited knowing, showing me the other side, which turned my ego into a small island in a vast sea. I had to see some greater purpose for myself, or be submerged by the waves. As life revealed just how meaningless my little island was, I trembled in the vast sea of this universe.

First Doris, and then Genny, had taken me from the desolate shore of that lonely island of myself, to where the sea and I grew together. Meditation and dreams had led me. But it was both Doris' and Genny's unconditional love which had sparked my sense of purpose, awakening my heart to comprehend what was before me.

Now both Genny and I were being confronted with how limited our capacity to receive and give had been. The gentleness that comes through the mediums in trance beckons us to follow. The psychic surgery, the phenomenon of the Philippine healers, is like a giant flag reminding everyone that God's existence is the source of all healing. And God is available to the medium as he or she gives his entire being to be used for His presence. Here with Paz, religion was not abstract. Jesus, the disciples, the angels, and all the principalities of heaven were a literal force called upon and recognized with their pure hearts.

I remembered Alberto telling me that primitive tribes in Africa and some groups in South America channel the same energy, the same forces. Their descriptions of the spirits that come to them are exactly the same as those of the mediums in the Philippines, except that they do not necessarily use Biblical references. More and more we were being shown that healers in many different cultures draw upon the same energies. Depending upon the degree of openness of their hearts, they attract varying degrees of pure energy with which to heal.

As the week continued, in our resistance to meditating every three hours the boredom and impatience surfaced. I saw the part of me which was so dependent upon phenomena, which required a vision or some specific peaceful feeling to make my meditation a success. It was as if I needed candy to make life sweet instead of knowing its sweetness naturally. I couldn't just know His essence. I wanted to be able to taste Him. I saw how I was needing constant reinforcement to affirm my progress.

Meditating in the early morning hours and the simple life in the village were urging us to return to our greater Self. We had no distractions. Everything was gently reminding us to go within. We took walks every day. We held hands and watched the children watching us. People stood in doorways, in no hurry, smiling. The pace of life was so seductive to our spirits. It had none of the pressures which usually consume so much of our attention.

Our dreams of being in a foreign culture to seek a spiritual life were unfolding. We saw how television, newspapers, and movies—all the distractions of our own familiar culture—had occupied so much of our consciousness, taking important space away from God. By removing ourselves from the normal pursuits, routine chatter, and business which was taken for granted back home, we were feeling how much emptiness we too easily avoided or filled with everything but what really satisfies.

Ironically, as we experienced our dream coming true, nearly all the Philippinos we met talked about coming to America. Slowly we began to understand that the secrets we fantasized being held in far-away villages were right there within ourselves. The challenge in any culture is to pass through the distractions and tempting desires of our personalities to find the shared breath in each of us. Only then can we discover that there is one heart that beats in all of us, that everything is a part of God. The sense of purposefulness that this awareness was bringing to me in this hot, muggy village, was making all our experiences more and more related. I began to know with increasing certainty that each attempt to risk living the truth in some miraculous way affirmed the whole universe. All I wanted in these moments was to be wholly myself.

Chapter Ten

✦ ✦

On holy days and special occasions many people from the village came together to go on what they called "missions" into the mountains or other remote areas of the Philippines. They went to help the poor and the sick or to seek a vision or to receive a blessing from special teachers who lived in more primitive areas.

Only days after our arrival we were invited to go on one of those special missions, one which others had been praying for and waiting for, for many months. We met early in the morning and joined the others at the church to pray for a safe journey. We would be traveling five or six hours back into the mountains to visit with an old medium named Sister Rose. Everyone who spoke of her called her the White Rose, as a symbol of her purity. Paz explained that Sister Rose had been her teacher for many years. It was Sister Rose who had originally predicted our visit to Paz and the Philippines.

Each of us was told to spend time going within and become clear on our purpose for going on the mission. Some people talked about their desires for physical healing, advice, or direction in their lives. Genny and I decided we wanted to know our highest purpose. Why were we here?

We boarded the jeepney, an open bus. Each person assumed no more space than was absolutely necessary. There were twenty of us in a space meant for no more than ten or twelve.

As we slowly worked our way towards the mountains, Genny and I watched in awe as we passed the vast rice fields and tropical green forests. Some of the roads had been washed out from recent storms. Several times we were all asked to get out and walk alongside the jeepney, through streams rushing over the roads. We realized that praying for a safe journey was not an empty ritual. Genny and I began the day with that morning's lesson in the *Course*:

> *"Each day, each hour, every instant, I am choosing what I want to look upon, the sounds I want to hear, the witnesses to what I want to be the truth for me."*[60]

Along the way, Paz explained that there was no telephone nor any other means of communication where we were going. But, she reassured us, she had sent Sister Rose a message telepathically, telling her the day and approximate time of our arrival. When the jeepney finally struggled up the last dirt road to a cluster of huts, sure enough, the great White Rose stood in her doorway. She was peering through the rain, waiting for us. It had been an unusually heavy rainy season. It took nearly twenty minutes to walk fifty feet through thick mud from the door of the bus to Rose's hut, high on stilts.

Sister Rose was many inches shorter than five feet, and her presence was much greater than her 90 pounds. As she laughed and bowed hello to everyone, she commended us all for our courage in making the trip. She said that she hoped the rains would stop so that the next day she could make it to the church, which stood another hundred yards away. As the usual black tea and coffee was being offered, Genny asked to use the bathroom. She was directed to a back room. Genny entered the room indicated. It was completely empty. Through gaps woven in the bamboo floor, she could see the ground about four feet beneath her. There was no exit leading to anything outside. She came back and asked again, and they all laughed as they realized Genny's predicament. Someone tried to explain that the whole room was the bathroom. After squatting anywhere, one just throws some water on the floor, sending what you had left onto the ground below. Everyone seemed to enjoy our awkwardness.

Paz had begun to talk about Sister Rose. We were told she was always in another state of consciousness, and we should listen carefully to each word she said. When she went into full trance we would know it. Everyone was speaking in a dialect native to this particular region of the Philippines. I listened as Paz translated for us.

Sister Rose turned to us after hearing our story from Paz. "You already had the powers and lost them. You will have everything you ask for and more. But you must not hold onto material things."

Her words remained in our thoughts, as we tried interpreting their meaning. We all went to bed early. It was cool. The rain had slowed down, and we made our way to the church. Its concrete floor was our bed. Our clothes were our blankets. I tried visualizing the floor as a green meadow in an attempt to get to sleep. I had only limited success. With the coming of daylight, however, we were surprised at how good we felt and how quickly our stiff backs and joints no longer concerned us. Before breakfast we were all told to give thanks and meditate, because another special medium had arrived in time for the service.

While waiting outside in the sunshine, we smiled as we watched Sister Rose pick her way towards the church with her cane. As she approached us, she apologized that her English was not very good. We were of course embarrassed, because we hadn't bothered to learn anything substantial of the various dialects which were spoken there.

We were told that this time with Sister Rose was valuable, and we should ask her anything we wished. I told her our story and the story of Doris, and asked her to send healing to Doris. Genny asked about her grandmother, in her eighties, who was back in the States.

"I will visit them both tonight," Sister Rose said. "I always work late at night when the air waves are not busy. Now we should talk about you."

She stood there, looking us over, and smiling. "You are to be blessed today with the mark and seal of the Holy Spirit. A 'Z' will be put on your foreheads so that everywhere you go, the Holy Spirit will know you." I wondered what it all meant. But the service was just about to begin, and we were being taken into the small church.

Besides our group, many other people were filling every corner of the building. The service began with everyone standing and singing. Someone nearby translated for us, explaining that this was the time everyone's prayers were answered, if they had not, in some mysterious way, already been satisfied. Sister Rose, Paz, and the other medium were up front. When each of them went into trance, we noticed that their voices changed, and a quiet excitement filled the air. Suddenly, petite Sister Rose appeared much larger than anyone in the room. She had the presence and power of a Moses. Her small voice was now a large wind filling the entire church. We didn't understand what was being said, but everything had changed. The audience grew quiet, held fast by the mediums' messages. They appeared to be consumed in fire, talking as if from the top of a holy mountain. As the audience continued to watch, one of the mediums announced that Acts 2, verses 1-4, confirmed the presence of the Holy Spirit. We turned to our Bible:

> "When the day of Pentecost had come, they were
> all together in one place. And suddenly a sound
> came from heaven like the rush of a mighty wind,
> and it filled all the house where they were sitting.
> And there appeared to them tongues as of fire,

*distributed and resting on each one of them. And
they were all filled with the Holy Spirit and began
to speak in other tongues, as the Spirit gave them
utterance."*

We sat there trying to integrate what we had felt
within us and the content of the Bible passage. Then
someone touched us and told us that we were being called
up front. The closer we got, the more we felt a power and
presence in the air that was almost overwhelming. I was
very conscious of each step as I walked closer. Someone
stood next to us and translated. "God protects those with
the seal of the Holy Spirit. With the reception of the seal,
you will feel His presence. All of the people of this world
who do have the sign of the Holy Spirit will meet each
other. You will automatically know one another. The Holy
Spirit feels that there are present those who will not feel
death. This power is on earth and is felt by those who
have the seal of the Holy Father."

Before I could understand fully what had just been
said, I became lost in my own experience. As the mediums
placed their hands over the Bible and under the banner
which hung loosely from the ceiling, I became unsteady. I
felt as if I were completely naked, with nothing between
me and God. I offered my will, my hopes, my darkness,
my love—everything I could offer. I gave all of myself to
His presence forever and ever.

At that instant of giving myself for all lifetimes, a
tremendous burst of energy passed through me. I was
ecstatic! I felt every atom of my body being filled with
strong waves of white light and love. I was observing
myself, and then I was inside myself. I felt as if I were
standing in the midst of grace, a state of forgiveness and
innocence. The next thing I knew I was kneeling. I looked
to my side and saw Genny and the other medium crying.
My body had been transported beyond a need for release
through tears. Holy cream was being rubbed into our
palms as we heard the words, "You are given the gift of
spiritual operation. Someday you will return for the power

of material operation, psychic surgery." The congregation was still standing and singing. "How much time had passed," I wondered.

Someone said to us, "You must pray that your worldly desires be lessened. You must focus on spiritual upliftment."

We were led to chairs, and people crowded around, smiling and congratulating us. Genny and I looked at each other and fell into each other's arms, crying. My mind was grasping for some way to integrate what had just happened. Instead, we simply held each other. I felt so empty, yet full, feeling as if I had just come into the world. I looked into Genny's eyes and knew that she also knew that the deepest essence of our individual beings had been united, fused into one purpose.

Later Genny described her experience during those long moments. "We were being blessed by fire. I felt I had been given the power of the Word. It had been placed within my hands to do God's work. Then a very peaceful feeling of light came over me. I was in a cave, receiving the gift of earth and nature from an intense light. The light was fire. I felt so weak. With all my remaining strength I gave thanks for the blessing. I prayed that I would do His will, hear His voice. I looked at my left hand and it was bright red in the center. It felt heavy, as if I were carrying a powerful tool. I looked over at Bruce and saw him kneeling before God. I felt we both were united as never before."

In the final stage of the experience, we were told to read the following passages:

> "God is spirit, and those who worship Him must worship in spirit and truth."—John 4:24
> " 'I am the Alpha and the Omega' says the Lord God, who is and who was, and who is to come, the Almighty."—Rev. 1:8
> "Then he showed me the river of the water of life, bright as crystal, flowing from the throne of God, and of the Lamb through the middle of the

street of the city; also, on either side of the river, the tree of life with its twelve kinds of fruit, yielding its fruit each month; and the leaves of the tree were for the healing of the nations. There shall no more be anything accursed, but the throne of God and of the Lamb shall be in it, and his servants shall worship him; they shall see his face, and his name shall be on their foreheads." —Rev. 22 verse 1-4.

The service ended. Sister Rose came up to Genny and me and hugged us. She said, "Read Psalms 23 and 27 often until we're back together again." She smiled and hugged us again.

Chapter Eleven

✦ ✦

After spending one more night on the church floor, we returned to Paz's home the next morning. Before we left, Sister Rose came over and told us that she had visited Doris last night. "She is very lonely," Sister Rose said, "but lots and lots of spirit helpers are with her. I gave her a spiritual gift for her heart." Then she turned towards Genny and began describing the exact location and layout of her grandmother's farm. Without knowing her grandmother's physical condition beforehand, Sister Rose said, "She had pain in her legs. I gave her injections. She was surprised by my presence there. I was strange to her, but she accepted the healing. I will continue to send her more."

Our apprenticeship was taking a new course. As we ate breakfast in Paz's kitchen, a young schoolteacher, with a severely swollen face, came to the door. I looked at the young woman and instantly knew Genny and I would work with her. Even as the thought came, Paz was speaking. "She has an illness of the spirit, not of the flesh. Doctors cannot help her. Holy Spirit directs you to work with her every three hours."

The day of healing continued. There was a woman with sore eyes, and another with an ear infection. Paz's niece also came. She had developed a high fever. Between healings, Paz taught us: "Illness has three causes," she said. "First, there are lower forces. Secondly, sometimes simple carelessness is the cause. The third cause of illness can be sins. We are not necessarily being punished by God, but our actions have consequences upon our own being. We are guided and affected by lower forces or higher forces, depending upon our thoughts. The body experiences the results of our attitudes. And our thoughts determine the quality of the forces which help guide us."

Paz's theory felt very comfortable, in that it eliminated the need to assign blame for illness, yet provided us with the concept that illness serves to remind us that our thoughts and behavior have consequences. Genny and I had already discussed this. We were attempting to not let our minds judge the reasons for illness but to let our hearts ask, "What is the blessing that this time can bring? Help me to recognize the Divine presence within each person, the Divine presence which comes in the disguise of an illness."

Even then we knew our work would be less and less about healing and more about supporting others as they came into their own experience of the Divine Self. The need for the illness, and the illness itself, disappears with the advent of that experience.

That night we worked again with Paz's grandmother, who was congested. Afterwards, Paz prayed and gave us the gift of spiritual injection. Genny and I were to place our right hand on the Bible, then we were to allow ourselves to feel the healing energy fill up an invisible syringe in our hands. We gave spiritual injections to the entire family. Everyone's faith helped us to trust our own inner guidance as to what part of the body to administer the injections. As I gained confidence and trust in my internal world, I felt my guide taking my hand and lifting my fingers to the place needing to be touched. My senses were talking to me from inside out, instead of collecting data from the world and bringing it to me. My guide's direction that Paz's brother was having breathing problems and digestion pains turned out to be correct. That voice within me was becoming louder, as I was becoming quieter and more accepting of its presence.

I knew that the medical influence in psychic healing was partly from the general shortage of physicians. Still, the metaphor of a spiritual injection has a special meaning. The healers have developed the discipline of imagining the most pure love of the universe filling an invisible syringe and injecting it into their patients. If healing is a question of in whom we place our faith, I loved living in a culture that believed in injections of spiritual love, instead of drugs. The imaginations of both healer and patient can have incredible effects when the patient actively becomes involved in receiving treatment as an act of receiving love. And if illness is essentially caused by lack of love, what better treatment could there be?

Paz explained the difference between spiritual injections and operations, where an invisible procedure is taking place, and material injections and operations, or psychic surgery, as it is called. Most healers begin performing spiritual healing. When their consciousness begins to see the invisible as concretely as it sees the visible, their injections may actually draw blood or, as in the case of the operations, the skin is literally pierced. In such cases, the existence of God's love has become a physical reality. The healer begins asking, "Why shouldn't the patient be feeling the injection or the operation as much as I feel the syringe or my hand reaching into their stomach."

After the healer spends more and more time in the consciousness of knowing, the love which guides his hands has fewer and fewer limits. As the healer opens up to the potential of unconditional love in general, the possibility of love changing physical matter is not such a great leap in consciousness. Genny and I were taking leaps in faith as we opened to the possibilities of love, as in an injection of love or as in an operation where love is restored to the body.

We were beginning to understand that the medical procedures were adopted not only to make up for the shortage of medical treatment but to give God an everyday reality as medicine is an everyday "reality." There was something very matter of fact about receiving a spiritual injection, very believable and very practical.

In the following days we were also introduced to spiritual x-rays, plain pieces of paper which had been held up to the body. The medium then asked to see the inner conflict or illness. Another medium took each patient's wrist and made an imprint with her finger, then read the patient's blood pressure with her clairvoyance.

At this time and place, doctors remain a scarcity, partly because there is little publicly funded medicine and partly because the people are relying more and more on their own inner resources. Meanwhile the medical societies and the government do not crack down on the healers because they recognize that they play a valuable role in meeting the needs of the poor, needs no one else is willing to serve.

Interestingly enough, some healers who had developed the gift of performing psychic surgery have returned to simply laying-on-of-hands. The parallels to medicine were ultimately unnecessary and perhaps too secular for such a sacred experience. Both Genny and I began to have similar feelings. What interested us was not only the psychic gifts of performing medical procedures without medical training and equipment but the potential awareness of the healer. Nowhere else was healing so clearly seen as more than treating physical symptoms, as also a process of restoring love and faith to the patient.

This was our inspiration. In the midst of poverty and disease, both the healer and the patients were communicating nothing more or less than the purity of innocence. Innocence, charity, and love were the cornerstones of each church. But most of all, innocence.

The lack of medical equipment meant to us the

absence of any distance between healer and patient. No drugs or herbs, no diagnostic labels, nothing but one's hands and open heart were parts of the healing relationship. In its simplicity, something unfathomable was taking place, something that could not be understood unless we directly experienced it ourselves.

Day after day, and night after night, we attended healing services of every imaginable kind. My neatly labeled packets of beliefs about the physical and spiritual world were being torn into disorder, until even my body began to show the effects of that breakdown. A fever again erupted. I did not know which language to think in. Was I still integrating our initiation by spiritual fire with Sister Rose? Was I resisting, frightened by the implications of my growing abilities? Or was I still fighting the fever of weeks before? Were malaria germs still running loose within me? As I lay in bed, I wondered which world I belonged to. My fever burned and burned into the night.

That night and the next day, whenever I opened my eyes, I found Paz on her hands and knees giving me a sponge bath of hot water and vinegar. Every three hours she reappeared beside my bed, bathing me, and praying for my spiritual development. I heard her asking for divine intervention, so that I would be well enough to go to church and participate in the healings the next day. I was hot, sweaty, smelling of vinegar, and embarrassed by the physicalness of my being, as Paz ministered to all my needs. She was changing the sheets, waiting on me, and hovering over me as if I were a garden of blooming flowers. My physical comfort was her only desire. After all the ceremonies, new experiences, and recent insights, I now saw the practicalities of what a healer really is. I felt humbled by her love.

Sure enough, I was in church when the service began at 8:00 in the morning. Everyone stood to sing. As the church's medium, Paz went into trance and delivered a message for the whole village. The spirit speaking through her quoted many books and verses from the Bible to substantiate the message. For the next few hours people went up front and talked to each other as if it were a village meeting. Everyone told of their adventures with God, their desires and experiences.

My body shuddered. I was hot and then cold as we sat there. There was constant motion around us—children, cats, chickens, and dogs coming and going.

At one point, the whole congregation stood again and marched to the front. They took all their valuables— wallets, purses, family treasures, even the food for dinner which they placed on a table. As everyone crowded around the table, Paz led them in a blessing, asking that our physical world lead us to our greater treasure in heaven. This was a weekly ritual. They gave thanks for their possessions, and asked that everything, including their debts, be blessed to serve some higher purpose. They spoke of reuniting their poverty with their true source of wealth.

It was now noon. The church became quiet again as the healing service began. Suddenly many more people were present. We were told that many villagers who belong to other churches, including some of the local Catholic priests, frequently slip in unobtrusively for a healing. Or as Paz said, with a slight chuckle, "They sneak in."

Paz and another healer set up a table on which people could lie down. Lines of twenty or thirty people began forming in front of Paz and the other healers. On one table, cotton and oil had been readied for the psychic surgery. Others were lining up in front of Paz. Paz motioned to Genny and me. We were asked to assist.

The church was literally drumming with all the energy and anticipation. Within moments, Genny had a line of people waiting to be worked with. Another line stood in front of me. As each person came forward, I was amazed by their openness and their expectation of healing. As I began reaching inside myself, surrendering and seeking to feel God's presence, my body began feeling stronger. Focusing on knowing and seeing only the purity of each person, I discovered that my own conflicts were receding. It was as if we were standing in a shower of light together. As long as we stood where we were, the light was the only reality. One at a time, people stepped into the shower with me. As each one entered, I saw a medicine cabinet hovering above our heads. For each person I saw a different bottle prominently displayed. In each instance, I knew that I was to take it and offer the invisible medicine to the person. No words were spoken. But between us, there was a deep understanding that we were all seeking the same truth.

A mother and child appeared, and I felt compelled to stand with both of them. I felt blessed by their union, the mother-child relationship that we all have with God.

A man came forward covered with sores from head to foot. Behind those wounds he seemed to be reaching out so intently. Something in me felt compelled to touch each sore as if I were about to behold a flower. I prayed that I could be with him as if I were standing in a garden. And when I held his feet, suddenly my mind jumped in. "Be careful! Someone who has all these sores is surely full of toxins. Do you want to hold his feet?" And at that instant my heart opened and something else in me said, "Yes. Yes." And I knew I was holding His feet. All I wanted in my life at that instant was to feel His love.

As we finished, I had tears in my eyes. I looked over to Genny and saw that her cheeks were wet as well. We reached for one another and held hands. I knew she was feeling what I felt. All we wanted was to be able to feel more and more of His love in everyone we met.

Twenty, thirty, forty people must have passed by us. The spot where we stood felt sacred. Instead of becoming more tired as I stood working, I got stronger and more invigorated.

Arm in arm, Genny and I took a long walk around the village, comparing our experiences. She, too, saw a medicine cabinet appear before her. She, too, felt more energy flowing through her as each person was healed. I felt each encounter was so complete even though I was with each person only moments, perhaps as long as two minutes. We had no real idea how much we had really served. Few words passed during that hour. In our brief times together we had just shared moments of truth, without explanation, unnecessary talk, or preparation. The healing that morning was much less about physical healing than about simply giving and receiving from one another. It was so clear that it was from this opportunity to serve that we felt expanded. On the other hand, the times I was waiting to be served, I knew how contracted I became. Why couldn't it always be this simple?

Upon arriving home, we saw Paz once again moving her belongings out of a room which she shared with two others. A man named Paul from the States was moving in. He was on crutches and had braces on his legs from an accident which resulted in a severed spine. He said that he had come to the Philippines as a last resort, to see if he could be healed.

As everyone was running around the house trying to prepare for Paul, Genny and I found ourselves getting annoyed with his seemingly casual attitude of expecting everyone to wait on him. Paz was oblivious to his behavior, trying to make him as comfortable as possible. Special meals were being planned for him, because he wanted to eat certain foods. Furniture was being moved, and healers were being sent messages. Meanwhile, Paul simply sat around in the living room. He seemed to be unconcerned, as if it were all being charged to his credit card. The whole house was being turned upside down and no one had any expectation of being paid anything.

Our inner peace was shattered. An American came into the middle of our idyllic spiritual healing apprenticeship, embarrassing us with his attitudes. And to make things worse, as Genny and I went outside to get away from the situation, we opened the *Course* and read:

> *"You cannot enter into real relationships with any of God's sons unless you love them all and equally. Love is not special."*[61] $T.-247$

Why did we randomly turn to this page in the book? Why did Paul appear in our lives on this day of all days? Of course we knew all of this wasn't just a coincidence. In our minds we tried to arrange things so that our uneasiness and judgments seemed more righteous, but the truth persisted.

In the following days we watched from the sidelines as Paz waited on Paul hand and foot, praying for him and taking him to see many healers. He admitted that he didn't believe in healing and wanted proof that it really worked. His constant requests were pleasantly met by various family members. When he sent someone out for more groceries or soft drinks, he offered to pay them only as a second thought.

Meanwhile Paz had gone into trance, and had been told by her guides that complete healing was possible for Paul. Paz was giving messages and hiring special vehicles to take him to healers. In the meantime she was sleeping on the concrete floor so Paul could have the last bed.

Our resentment was boiling. How could someone so irresponsible receive complete healing? Doesn't telling him that complete healing is possible only reinforce his arrogance? We were jealous that all of Paz's attention was directed elsewhere. We knew how ridiculously we were behaving. Why did we "choose" Paul, an American who had so many of the attitudes we are ashamed of, to move into the house in the middle of our apprenticeship? The more Paz gave and gave, the more we were humbled by her ceaseless energy. Paul, meanwhile, simply expected it, and asked for more. Days had now become weeks, and nothing seemed to change.

I'll never forget Paul's face as he watched Sister Josephine insert cotton into one part of a person's body and pull it out someplace else. Indeed, he had even looked over his shoulder and watched her as she stuck a large ball of blessed cotton into his lower back and left it there. He stood up and put his hand on the spot. Previously, that area of his back had no feeling, but now he felt some sensation there. Josephine had instructed him to leave the cotton in and return in a week so that she could pull it out. Paul was incredulous, thinking about the ball of cotton still inside his back. As the week wore on, he seemed to think less and less about the cotton and Sister Josephine. When the day came for him to return to Sister Josephine, it rained so hard that it was impossible to make the trip. Paul became anxious. We could tell that he was thinking, "What if that cotton is there, and I never get it out?" He wanted to go to another healer to have her check to see if there really was cotton stuck inside of him.

Without telling anyone of his plans, he made his way to a local healer who did not have the gift of cleansing the body with cotton. He asked if she saw anything in his back. The healer prayed, looked at him and said, "Why yes, you have cotton in your back." And she removed a wad of cotton from exactly the same place Josephine had placed it a week before. Paul was astonished. After he recovered he was relieved that the cotton had been removed. It was only hours, however, before he again began doubting the whole series of events.

He knew that the healers were not involved in this for the money, because he saw how poor everyone was. Even though they made great efforts in coming to see him, they never once asked him for money. He insisted the sensations he had begun feeling in his legs and back were not proof enough. One night he started getting muscle spasms in one leg which had had no feelings for many months. But for him this wasn't adequate proof of potential healing.

The next morning we were with another healer who had given Paul a spiritual injection. As we all watched, his knees began to bleed slightly. They seemed to be bleeding from the invisible needle which had been directed there. Paul stood and watched. We all did. Within hours, however, he had again decided that he hadn't really seen what he thought he had.

From our serene Philippine journey, we were thrown back into our Western selves. The *Course* seemed to lecture us each step of the way:

* * *

"Those who see themselves as whole make no demands."[62] *"What you perceive in others you are strengthening in yourself."*[63] W . 56 T. - 73

We knew we had let Paul become a distraction from our work. As all our judgments glared at us, Paz's constant unconditional love reflected back to us our lack of commitment. Yet we still held fast to our belief that healing can take place only when the patient begins to give. We decided to move out of the house.

We told Paz about our feelings. At first she was hurt. A friend interceded and explained that we just wanted more time and space to continue our own training. Paz quickly understood our need and blessed us.

We then began training three mornings a week with another healer in a nearby town. Each day, after a brief service, we would work with about twenty to thirty people. Our feelings of knowing the softness and directness of the Holy Spirit were building almost daily. It was a forty-minute bus ride to the healer's small church, which was basically a concrete shell with a few benches in it. A partial roof was still being built. During the ride was a perfect time to read the *Course* and prepare:

"Put all your faith in the love of God within you; eternal, changeless, and forever unfailing. This is the answer to whatever confronts you today."[64] W. 79

The days that we resisted rising early and making the trip, we knew were the most important days to go. Each day, we would meditate on the way over, asking over and over in our minds, "May my thoughts be Your thoughts, my heart be Your heart, my hands be Your hands." After the service on the days we most wanted feedback about whether or not we really were helping anyone, we heard nothing. And on the days when God's presence was undeniable reality that needed no one else's confirmation, many people would approach us afterwards saying, "Remember me from last week? Remember my back? Well, it's been just fine!"

It was on such days that the whole world again seemed to be clapping for us. The *Course* echoed the feeling:

> *"It is quite possible to reach God. In fact, it is very easy, because it is the most natural thing in the world."*[65] W. 44

It all felt so right.

> *"Where God is, there are you. Such is the truth."*[66]
> T. -270

All this time, Paul was still living in Paz's home. Despite the many healings and flurry of activity around him, his condition had changed very little. There was some improvement, but his doubts were as persistent as his condition. As Genny and I watched and prayed, we were resolved to continue to leave the whole affair in God's hands. Even with our differences, we were becoming friends with Paul. We had to admit that Paz's love had made him more gentle and easier to get along with. Paul was even developing a sense of humor about all the fuss in caring for him.

He rarely sought our opinion about what we saw happening. One morning, he did, however. "If healing is real," he asked, "why would it take more than one healing for someone to get well?"

"Each time someone approaches a healing," I explained, "hopefully they are becoming more and more open to accepting God's love."

"But," he said, "doesn't everyone want complete healing the first time?"

"Yes," I said, "everyone probably wants complete healing. At least in their minds they do. But their hearts may not be ready to receive. They may have many doubts preventing them from receiving it."

Genny became involved then and said, "Paul, simply putting your body on the table in front of a healer is not the answer. God is also within you. As you make decisions and assume responsibility, God can work through your efforts."

"What we are saying," I interrupted, "is that no one, as far as we know, is healed without being involved themselves, by trusting and risking that healing is possible."

We all admitted that there was no simple explanation or answer. Nevertheless, Paul chose to continue to try every healer who came along. And we decided to let go of our investment in his getting well.

Since we had had no reprieve from our inward discipline for weeks, we decided that it was time for a retreat. We needed to relax and stop taking ourselves and everything else so seriously. The China Sea was only a half-day's bus ride away. Since it was not the tourist season, the resorts on the beach were practically empty. We were alone as we waded out into the water at sunset and offered our souls to His Kingdom.

The *Course* said:

"When you want only love you will see nothing else."[67] T.-215

And love was all we felt.

The next morning we hired a small dinghy and a guide to take us out to a reef to snorkel. We had been rowing across the calm ocean for about an hour when we noticed the sky slowly turning black. A large storm was coming towards us. We pulled up the anchor and started back to shore, fearing it could be only minutes before the storm was upon us. Genny and I looked at each other from opposite ends of the boat as the guide concentrated on his rowing. There would be no way for this boat to survive the waves. Could we return in time? We looked at him and again at each other. A strange feeling suddenly washed over me, and I knew Genny had had the same thought at that same instant. Why would God bring us all the way to the Philippines to drown in a storm? It made no sense. Of course we would be protected. As we watched our guide paddle us to shore, we watched the Holy Spirit keep the storm at bay. At the exact moment we scrambled from the boat onto the beach, a mightly wind began to drive mountainous waves, such as we had never seen, against the resort.

We hurried back to our hotel room and sat there as the building shook with the storm's intensity. We lit a candle and gave thanks. Perhaps for the first time, we really understood the difference between having faith in God and knowing God. We read in the *Course* that evening:

> *"To think like God is to share His certainty of what you are, and to create like Him is to share the perfect Love He shares with you."*[68] *"With love in you, you have no need except to extend it."*[69] T. 105 T. 292

❧❧

Chapter Twelve

✦✦

Paz had warned us before our retreat not to drink alcohol or see any movies. We ignored her advice, however, thinking it was mainly her Catholic values. We seldom drank anyway, and we wanted a change in routine, so we did go to the only movie in the area. It turned out to be a poor murder mystery. Afterwards, we were surprised at how upset we were. At home we had been to many similarly low-grade entertainments and went about our evenings unaffected. Why was it so different now?

That night we both had nightmares. We slept very little, feeling vulnerable and under attack. Maybe all the reading of the Psalms, asking that we be cleansed, had had some effect. All that day and the next we felt dulled and emotionally misshapened by the film's effects. We began to have more respect for the potential of movies to stimulate mental activity. We also began to glimpse the enormous amount of everyday psychic input that we took for granted at home, something we had seldom even acknowledged, let alone comprehended.

What did this say about everyday mental activity in

the West? I wondered, if one film had had such effect on us, would we all too easily slip back into the urban pollution of mental traffic which is normal back home? Would we lose the inner peace we had found? At least half of our apprenticeship had been involved with learning how to unwind and not be preoccupied and entertained all day long. Life in the lowlands had been little more than meditation, long walks, listening to the pouring rain, a nap, meals of rice and some meat, and, every few days, meeting and working with different healers. Every part of each day affirmed our purpose here. Once accustomed to the abundance of time on our hands, we could feel our minds let down their shields. The volume of mental energy we generally receive, process, and exchange had slowed to a mere trickling stream.

Meanwhile, what had been mind-altering or utterly unbelievable a few weeks ago was almost becoming ordinary. Psychic surgery was no longer a phenomenon separate from the normal spiritual atmosphere in the village. We now felt that packing cotton into one part of the body and pulling it out from another part, days later, was a perfectly natural way of healing. Only when we tried to understand intellectually what was happening or how it was happening did we find ourselves literally becoming dizzy and disoriented to the point of having to leave the room to regain our balance.

One day we found ourselves only a few feet from a healer, watching her pull yard after yard of gooey string out of a woman's stomach. Then she reached into the abdomen of another person and pulled out a plastic bag. Both cases were explained as cases of black magic, where people were "possessed" in a bizarre way by someone's bad wishes for them.

We were told by a European researcher that a Philippino physician told her that he knew of a patient with a similar complaint. Evidently, a healer told this person that a plastic bag was in his stomach and should be removed. The patient resisted and went to a traditional physician instead. The doctor did exploratory surgery to find the cause of the intense pain, and pulled out a plastic bag from the man's stomach.

These stories presented a big challenge when we tried to view them out of the context of a culture in which people believe in God and also believe that the power of harmful thoughts is as real as any physical object they can see and touch. These are people who are intimately involved daily with forces beyond themselves, forces which nevertheless seem natural to them.

The President of Paz's church had become a close friend. One day he laughingly related the story of how he had been converted to Espiritism. It happened quite rapidly, as rapidly as the movement of a psychic surgeon's hands when he pulled a piece of pink negligee from a man's stomach, as his wife and family watched.

At the time he didn't believe in mediums, spirits, or anything remotely related. All that had interested him was his work and his playboy lifestyle. But as he watched a healer who did not know his lifestyle pull a piece of filmy nylon negligee from his lower belly, suddenly his life caught up with him. And the constant pains and discomfort in his stomach area began to have reality-shattering meaning. He could no longer run from the truth about himself. Also, he could no longer deny the truth of the Espiritistas' way and the need for something greater in his life. Psychic surgery was a means to return to his family and rethink his life's direction.

As we watched the healers work, we realized more and more that they really were skilled therapists. A forgiving, all loving God was offered, instead of conflict and disbelief. Each patient's surrender to something greater than himself mobilized a force within, affirming each person's essential wholeness. The weight of his illness, or mental or emotional darkness, invariably lifted.

Something in me knew that when a blind man dies, he sees again. When a paralyzed man dies, he walks again. Someone in terrible pain on death's bed is free of the pain once he has passed on. His experience is that of his spirit, which is always whole. Each healer we were meeting was simply practicing seeing the wholeness as existing now. The healers were seeing the completeness of the spirit as the only reality. With God in their hearts they saw a vision of each person as pure and already perfect. The healing methods they used were their attempts to demonstrate God's already existing love by restoring the body of physical wholeness.

We continued visiting Old Man Eduardo in his small barn on Thursday evenings. At one of those meetings, his guides had told us to go to a different church each Sunday for three weeks. In each of those communities we were overwhelmed by the warmth and receptivity of the people toward the Westerners coming in to participate in their service. Their humble churches were filled with laughing children and farm animals running loose in the aisles, and the adults were as simple and open as the children.

Only in Baguio, a town in the hills above the tropical heat and humidity, did we find the healers and their communities influenced by the typical attitudes we had come to associate with any organized religious group. Bagiuo was most known for its famous healers who treated busloads of tourists who came all the way from parts of Asia and Europe to the Philippines to receive healing. One healer, who had worked with people from all over the world, was now running a center where patients came and stayed for a week or longer. It was filled with gossip and conflict. In his climb to recognition and material success, it was said that he had fallen from the holy mountain and no longer had his gift of healing. Because of this, healers from the lowlands had been hired to work in the chapel.

This man was planning to open an even larger resort nearby, complete with modern pools and deluxe accommodations. Many doubted that the new building would ever be home to the same healing powers as before.

Is success inherently an obstacle? I had to ask myself if I'd ever met a wealthy man with humility. I thought of my own father, who may be the closest to such a person. His essential thankfulness and enjoyment of life is characterized by his attitude towards others. He rarely sees anyone else as basically different than himself. Perhaps it's that simple.

While our egos tempted us to work in Bagiuo with the more well-known healers, it was in the churches in the lowlands that we found ourselves surrendering most to the gentle spirit. It was in their simplicity that we knew they were blessed.

As the *Course* said:

> *"To be in the Kingdom is merely to focus your full attention on it."*[70] $T. - 108$

In the lowlands, we were as accepted as other healers were, but our minds were busy erecting defenses, disbelief, and sheer skepticism along the way. As the island of my ego was flooded from the overwhelming presence of the spirit, I saw myself, as if huddling by a tree, trying to figure out why my island was disappearing. At various times all through the summer, different healers had repeated similar prophesies. "You will begin a healing center attended by people from beyond your own surrounding area. Certain people will step forward and become pillars of support for your church. You will travel and train many others. The magnetism in your hands will grow until your touch lifts illness of all kinds." The words were so reinforcing to hear, yet they were empty and unempowered unless we gave them our belief.

One prophecy, I remember, said that Genny and I are always to be together. It is in our spiritual purpose that we will build our relationship. And if we ever lose that purpose, we will lose the relationship. Then I was told that if such an event happened, I would die shortly, because I would have no reason to remain. Something about those words pierced my hardened ego, allowing me to accept the truth that ultimately I have no choice but to risk and allow my heart, indeed my entire self, to serve, despite the frequent despairing wish to return to being "normal" like everyone else.

The healers had nothing to really hold onto as a source of stability. The weather, their government, and the random and seemingly capricious forces of their lives, provided no security. No matter how much I romanticized the notion, I feared attempting to live a life based on such a thin and fragile substance as trust. Yet I saw that even my relationship with Genny hung by such a thin and fragile thread, as we learned to depend on our faith, trusting our experience to be true.

One Sunday we were presented with two distinctly different lessons on how to build a life based on such a level of trust. The day started with our visit to a church where we had been working. At the end of the service, Genny and I were honored when the church's oldest member was brought to meet us. The frail old woman dressed in white sat in a chair in front of us and asked us to pray for her. I closed my eyes, and silently, with the voice of my heart, I asked her spirit to pray for all of us because it was so obvious that she was closer to living the truth. Her advanced age had turned physical life into spiritual wisdom. The body was not slowly decaying but transforming into spirit. She sat there as if she were seeing everything through her closed eyes.

When we returned home, we found Paul in bed. He had just returned from seeing another healer. He had not wanted to go, but since everyone was going, he went anyway. As usual, he had gone forward for healing. The healer rubbed some heavily scented oil into his legs. At the time it was painful, but Paul didn't complain, thinking it might do some good. He put his braces on again and returned home. By the time he had reached his room, each of his legs had erupted into a mass of blisters.

Paz had always said that she was only to serve and leave judgment to God. I thought about this when Paul was lying there, in intense pain, unable to move. Genny and I felt so badly for him. We recognized in ourselves that part of us which would try anything to make things right, instead of simply listening within. We could no longer judge Paul, but we couldn't help but judge ourselves. Would it have been best to abandon all of our feelings about Paul and leave him to his own path? Or should we have risked and communicated to Paul, from the beginning, just how deep our concerns were about his assuming responsibility with the healers?

We didn't know. Each of us plays a role in healing, and our role is no accident. At least we learned that when we have strong feelings about something, they are meant as teachers for everyone involved. Too often, either we think our feelings are only about ourselves or we react the opposite way, thinking our feelings have to do only with someone else. Healing does not happen in isolation from others any more than we can expect others to change in order for us to feel better. Life is such a balance—learning when to go within ourselves for healing and when to express ourselves in the world.

Paul had placed his body upon virtually every healer's bench, but he had yet to offer his heart. His suffering continued as he lay in bed for several days. Finally he said, "I know it's time to go home. I am not going to get well physically, at least not now, but I am getting well spiritually." The day he reached this resolution, he had a distinct calmness about him.

Paz and her family continued to serve him until his legs had healed enough to wear his braces. They even made the long trip to the airport in Manila to say goodbye.

We had completed our three Sundays away in different churches in the lowlands as Old Man Eduardo's guides had asked. We returned to his barn for guidance about the next steps in our training. There was only a brief service before he went into trance. Immediately his guide began to speak with a message for Genny and me. "You have now earned the trip to visit Eduardo's teacher."

We weren't certain what he meant. When the old man was told what had come through him while in trance, he became very excited. He was honored that he could introduce us to his teacher, whom he had described as a special old man. We were told that his teacher lived a full day's difficult ride over muddy roads far back into the mountains. Eduardo's enthusiasm alerted us. There was probably another purpose for making the trip.

Before he closed the service, Eduardo again entered trance and telepathically informed his teacher that we were coming and when to expect us. There was no other means of communication because of the rainy season. Besides, Genny and I had already observed the reliability of this communication system, which was practiced by the Espiritistas. We knew we would be expected.

Word of the planned journey spread quickly through the church. The challenge of the trip seemed to give it even more spiritual significance. If the rains came while we were enroute, it was likely we would be marooned in the mountains for some time. But Old Man Eduardo wasn't concerned. He knew his guides would not tell him to make the trip unless it were meant to happen. On the day of our departure, we met at the church for a brief ceremony before squeezing into the jeepney. Eduardo told us that the safest way to make the journey was to remain in silence and prayer. Otherwise, the effects of the hills and bumpy roads and other less visible forces on us could negatively influence the trip. Eduardo and many of the others seemed to have done additional spiritual preparation as well.

We had no idea what lay ahead. During the long ride, Genny and I held hands and had no trouble remaining quiet. The wild stories we had heard about Eduardo and his teacher filled our heads with lots to imagine.

Eduardo's teacher's story began before the Second World War when he had visited an Espiritista Church with a friend who was a member. It was his first experience of anything outside Catholicism. The medium, in trance, called him by name. Surprised and intrigued, he went forward. The medium drew a map and then warned him to take his family to the spot indicated or they would never survive the coming war.

He did not believe in mediums and was there only because his friend had invited him. How could a complete stranger know him by name? Why was this stranger saying that he must take his family to a cave hidden in the midst of some distant mountains now, before anyone was giving serious thought to a Japanese invasion?

In spite of his feeling that a Japanese threat seemed very remote at the time, he was compelled to at least look for the cave. The medium had had such a profound effect on him that he took his family back into the hills. He found the cave which turned out to be one of a series of caves. To his surprise, not only were they where the medium had said they would be but they appeared to have never been discovered. We were not told what he found in the caves, only that for all these years he has remained there.

The jeep ride could have been torturous. However, when we reached Eduardo's teacher, instead of feeling cramped and miserable from all the hours of riding on washed-out dirt roads, we were surprised at how well we felt. Instead of twenty people packed into one vehicle, it seemed as if only one had occupied the car.

Eduardo's teacher had been waiting for us on the side of the road, but he hadn't been waiting long. Eduardo matter-of-factly said that he had sent telepathic messages, letting his teacher know we would be arriving later than we had first expected. We unloaded the jeepney with great relief and were immediately led up a hill to a little chapel. Eduardo and his teacher immediately began a worship service. Within minutes, we met the spirit guide of Eduardo's teacher. Most Philippine mediums have a wide range of entities speak through them. But when Eduardo's teacher went into trance, only the spirit of Christ came through him. Eduardo stated simply, "He has opened his heart. He has asked to serve only the 'One Master.' "

While the boundaries of our belief system were trying to adjust themselves, we were overtaken by the sweet softness which we felt. There was such a simple manner about this old man. Genny pointed to a figure dressed in white which had appeared in front of him. The scent of roses and the touch of an incredible, but defined, presence filled the chapel. We had grown accustomed to the healers' belief that Jesus' disciples were not figures in history but living spiritual entities serving the earth. But talking about the living Christ and actually feeling His presence were two entirely different experiences.

The old man extended his arms, and for a moment I did not see him. Jesus Christ was the only one speaking. He was the only one in the room.

We were called forward. We kneeled. We were told, "You may ask any question."

Independently, both Genny and I had arrived at the same question as we remained fixed in that spot. "How can we best prepare for our spiritual work?"

But before we could ask, we heard his voice already answering our thoughts. Only a few moments later, neither of us could remember his words. An awareness of being held so closely to God and feeling, strangely enough, that God needed us as much as we needed Him, surprised and overtook our minds.

That night we slept on the hard benches in the chapel. Eduardo announced that his teacher had been given permission by his spirit guide to take us to the caves the next day. Genny and I lay awake most of the night, just trying to hold onto the feeling. Neither of us had ever felt so wanted, so purposeful, so in touch with ourselves before.

Everyone was up by sunrise. They were out in the morning air preparing for the day. Eduardo and the old man had risen early to go to the caves. The old man waited for us there while Eduardo returned to guide us. It was a short hike of less than a half a mile. As we wound around low hills, reaching the caves so soon was completely unexpected. The cave's entrance was perhaps thirty feet high. Eduardo taught us "how" to enter. Our whole group stopped at the entrance and began a short service. There was an immediate sense that this place should be respected as a sacred spot. Each of us silently sought permission before entering. We knew that unless we were absolutely clear about our purpose, we wouldn't be invited in.

The ceremony at the cave's entrance prepared us for what we found within. We understood immediately why this man had decided to spend his life here. This was not a damp, cold cavity in which we stood. We had walked into a holy place which the earth herself was protecting.

Hundreds of individual rays of light lit up the sides of the cave. We could not make out the source of the light. The floor was perfectly dry. The ceiling rose fifty feet above us. Descending from it were what appeared to be light beings, luminescent bodies filled with rays of sunlight.

We walked further back into the cave. Here, a whole series of caves honeycombed together. We made one more turn, and there stood Eduardo's teacher. He was already in trance. Today was a special day. As a sign of respect, he rarely went into trance inside the caves. He stood before us with his arms extended and his hands turned upward, as if inviting each of us into the kingdom. He stood there for a long silent moment. As a simple messenger of God, his presence was everything that could possibly be said.

That day, no questions or specific requests were to be made. He approached us, then bent over and gently touched our foreheads. Neither of us had expected what was to follow. Even now there are no words we can gather to describe the experience in its entirety. But as we turned around, we looked into a natural formation of rocks and saw a vision of history, purpose, and the life of mankind which has never left us.

There, carved by nature on one great wall of the cave, was a tapestry of faces and figures which came out of the wall, as if beckoning us. At the top in the center was a sea of faces filled with all extremes of emotion, as if representing all of life. A figure of Christ, with tears of pain and joy flowing down his cheeks, was in the middle. He was being helped down from the cross. As the figure was being lowered, it changed from the body of an old man, to that of a younger man, to a figure of a still much younger man, until at the bottom appeared a child climbing upwards towards the ultimate fate of the crucifixion. On either side of the child were several figures with their backs to us, bowing towards the Christ. On either side of the bowing figures stood a lamb and a lion, surrounded by many other animals. Their bodies were contorted with anger and fear, but at the same time filled with strength and light.

The more we looked into the sculpted rocks, the more we saw. All of mankind's pain was being lifted down from that cross and transmuted, until it became as a child standing among the animals. We saw man on his journey from the natural beauty of childhood into all walks of life. This led him toward the ultimate confrontation—the human and the divine meeting in the form of Christ being lowered from the Cross. Individual life and the history of all life was interconnected.

Images of great masterpieces of European art briefly flashed through my mind. It was as if the great masters had somehow known the secrets of this place and had been compelled to try to capture it on paint and canvas, in marble and bronze. Our journey—mankind's, Genny's, mine—began and ended in this cave. No possible human experience, between the misery of the descent and the peaceful humble figures in the garden at the base, was excluded. We enter this life, from God, to grow to the limits of our human nature. Then we surrender, return, and are held once again in the arms of love. What else is there?

We walked back and forth in front of the carvings, looking at the world from every possible angle. Then it occurred to us that we, indeed each soul, has experienced all of history, and is simply caught in this cycle of human divinity. We all are somewhere between birth and death, growing towards the awareness of how we are all related, of how we in fact share the same journey.

Genny and I stood transfixed in time. It seemed hours but it must have been only minutes. We were describing what we were seeing, as someone translated for the group. Eduardo and the old man were smiling. There was so much to see, and a part of us knew we would never fully comprehend what was in front of us. Everyone gathered for another ceremony, this time one of thanksgiving. As we went to join them, Genny and I were again thinking as if with one mind. Genny said, "I feel everything ending here, and we are starting again." I nodded. "I feel we came to the Philippines, to Paz, to Eduardo, and to this cave for ourselves, but as we leave, we know our purpose. We are leaving to serve others."

Chapter Thirteen

➤ ✦

Before we left, Eduardo's teacher came to us, "Remember," he said, "God knows your needs even before you do." He came closer to us. "The more you serve others, the easier it is for Him to care for you." He then embraced us and gave us a prediction. "You will someday return with a group; and Genny," he said, "will paint what she has seen in the cave."

The trip home was easier. Whether it was because of better road conditions or because a part of us was still inside the caves, I don't know. During the following days, we walked, meditated, and talked endlessly about the carvings. Were they really as we remembered seeing them or had we been in another state of consciousness? Had we been induced into an altered state of consciousness just by being with the old man? Is that why the carvings appeared to be so perfect? The images seemed greater than life. It was hard to fully believe that the carvings were as specific and detailed as we saw them. Yet how could we doubt our vision, when both of us saw exactly the same things so clearly shaped in stone?

The old man was perhaps the greatest mystery. Was it tragic or justly appropriate that someone who had reached such a state of elevated awareness would remain virtually unknown except by a very few? Then the thought came, as if placed in our minds: perhaps his prayers and his living in the caves have some effect upon the world, an effect much greater than we imagine.

As Genny and I began our walk, we looked at each other. Suddenly we looked again and were startled, as we noticed for the first time how thin we both had become. Each of us had lost fifteen or twenty pounds since our arrival. In addition to physical weight, we had also lost the incalculable weight of our persistent egos.

We had already recognized that we eat much more at home because of our need to fill ourselves spiritually. Our diet here had been rice, more and more rice, and only occasionally a little meat and some vegetables and fruit. But here there had been no temptation to fill ourselves in any way but spiritually. We could see how a simplified life, one that might almost be called poverty, could truly inspire one to greater heights. I realized how wrong we can be in the West, arrogantly thinking that because our plates are full, we have everything, and the rest of the world is without. We can no more judge others by their poverty than they can assume that all Westerners are wealthy and therefore happy.

Now Genny and I looked as if we too had nothing, and soon we would be returning to a world where everyone was seeking to have it all. In our loss of weight, we felt very thin emotionally as well. We both realized we had let go of more than we thought. What were we going to return with? We had some incredible stories, but our experiences felt too personal and too fantastic to share easily. If we only had something tangible to take home with us, something to help bridge the chasm between the two cultures. It was as if in following a trail into a magical land, we had forgotten how to return. We wanted to leave and return home. But how dull it would be in comparison. No—how unreal it would seem.

We ended up at Paz's home after our walk. She went into trance and gave us a "progress report" of our apprenticeship. She predicted that we would go home with all of her psychic and spiritual gifts. We knew, of course, that many of these would be with us, but they were in the infant stage, needing development. These and many more skills were being awakened in us. By gradually opening our hearts, we were told by Paz's guides, the gifts of the spirit come naturally. "As you help others to open to their real selves, remember you cannot force a heart to open, but know it will bloom with gentle care. As you help others to grow their gardens, your purpose will become clearer and clearer."

We were so fortunate to have had Paz as our teacher. Since we had experienced being with other healers, we had recognized that many had the gift of healing but not necessarily the gift of teaching and training. Paz is one of the few teachers in the Philippines who helps train healers. She taught us much about spiritual gardening—how people's gifts grow naturally in the right environment and right soil.

Paz was still in trance when she asked for a sheet of paper. She began scribbling on the page. She seemed to be drawing a picture of a flag similar to the banners that hung in the church. As she continued drawing, she said, "A banner is to be made for you, white with green trim. The words 'Divine' and 'Spiritual' are to be sewn across the top. In the middle is to be a yellow torch with the words 'work of charity' fixed around the flame. Underneath the torch, a Bible is to be stitched with the words 'God is Love' in bold print within it."

Paz's guides, still speaking through her, then told us, "This flag is to be blessed and will make your church a sister church to the Espiritista's in the Philippines. If you honor the words in the flag, the purpose of your work, including never turning anyone away, but truly do work of charity; and if you teach that God is Love, your lives will be protected and every need you may have will easily be satisfied."

Our own flag! We had asked for something tangible to bring home to remind us of our experiences. So the Holy Spirit designed a flag for us. It was all so perfect.

Paz showed signs of coming out of trance. But suddenly she turned towards Genny, and another voice began to say, "You are to be initiated as a medium. In three weeks you are to be given the seal of mediumship. This seal of protection is to be given by either three or seven mediums. It is a seal to bless you and protect you from anything but higher spirits speaking through you. You must meditate more and prepare yourself to be used in the service of mediumship."

Genny and I were aghast. For several months we had seen Philippine healers go into trance. It never occurred to either of us that someone else would speak through one of us. We left Paz's home and tried to integrate this totally unexpected prophecy.

We understood that everyone is a medium of sorts, meaning that everyone channels energy. Thoughts are like radio waves going everywhere in the universe. Most people, however, do not take responsibility for their thoughts, thinking they have no consequence. We normally don't realize that our thoughts determine the quality of our lives, our relationships, even the condition of the earth. Most people do not go through the discipline of raising the level of their thoughts. Instead they channel everyday thoughts and frequencies.

What discipline is necessary to become a medium? Meditation is only part of the training. We knew that loving, forgiving, and finding acceptance of our own conflicts was the bottom line. Hearing that Genny was to become a medium stirred up a lot for both of us to find peace with. Genny was certain that she did not want just anybody who had died to speak through her. She wanted only true teachers, teachers with a refined and enlightened consciousness.

We realized that most psychics have opened their minds to other frequencies. It is a rare psychic who has fully opened his heart as well. For the healers, the same is true. There are psychic healers who have opened to mental energy for healing. But the difference between psychic healing and spiritual healing is the difference between using our minds and using our hearts. In all cultures, mediumship varies depending upon the quality of energy, or most importantly, the quality of love that the medium has opened to.

Genny's mind, meanwhile, was spinning. Studying mediumship and actually surrendering to the experience were two different things. Genny asked, "When it takes over, where do 'I' go during the experience?" Neither of us knew.

Paz said, "Meditate. Quiet your mind. Ask to be of service. You will know if it's a higher spirit. If you feel the energy first in your right hand, your heart, or your forehead, you know you are being touched by a true teacher. If you feel the energy in your left hand, your stomach, or at your back, you know it is lower energy."

Genny had until Thursday evening to prepare herself. She had no idea what to expect. Paz's assurance that only a spirit with a high purpose would come through comforted both of us. Many other cultures and groups believe mediumship is an end in itself, regardless of the quality and peacefulness of the energy being channelled. Doris had already told us that there are a lot of people involved in some form of mediumship who end up with lost spirits who create physical, emotional, and spiritual damage.

I felt like an expectant father. I had no idea how it would be until Genny actually had the experience. I could support her, but like a woman pregnant, she was alone in this experience. With Thursday looming before her, it seemed as if her whole being were being tested. Any last ripple of fear of the unknown was destined to still surface.

Thursday evening came quickly. Genny was calm and prepared. I was incredibly nervous and excited. I was running around with a tape recorder, as if Genny were about to give birth and I wanted to record every moment. It was one thing to see others go into trance, and another to imagine Genny letting go of her mind to the point of having someone else using it and speaking through her.

As she surrendered to another level of service, I couldn't help but wonder what effects mediumship would have on our relationship. A whole new door was being opened. Like a new father, I was feeling pangs of jealousy toward the new baby. I was afraid of losing Genny to something else. Mediums in the Philippines go in and out of trance as a way of life. I had no idea where we were being led. Yet in the midst of my emotional chaos, something deep within me knew that everything was right. It was happening just as it was meant to be.

It began. Paz was standing up front facing the congregation. Genny was called to sit next to her. Everyone became quiet. But Genny had already moved deeply into her own peacefulness. It wouldn't have mattered if there were one person with her or a hundred. I didn't know whether to meditate, pray for the highest spirit to come to her, or to just watch proudly as she went further and further into the quiet recesses of her spirit. I could only watch and listen. I was much too excited to be of any spiritual support.

We all leaned forward as Genny at last began to speak. Her words were barely audible. As she sat there, eyes closed, body in complete and relaxed surrender, the presence in the room grew more powerful. She talked about inner peace and love, and then paused.

Then Paz abruptly interrupted her. "Wipe your forehead," she said, "and go sit down and pray."

"What happened?" we both simultaneously asked. "What's wrong?" Genny continued.

"You became afraid. Lower energies were about to come to you," Paz said. "Sit down and meditate and pray."

After a few minutes, Genny had again centered herself. She described what had happened. "I was becoming a part of a powerful energy that seemed to envelop me. At first I felt it only in my heart and my right hand. There was so much energy I couldn't even move my right hand.

Then in one instant everything shifted. I had one thought and then with the speed of another thought, I questioned what was happening to me. The next thing I knew Paz was telling me to sit down."

One of the church members who was clairvoyant said she had seen a beautiful spirit standing just to the side of Genny, but Genny's thoughts must have changed, because another presence entered the room. The new spirit was not evil but much heavier, with no special qualities. The service had ended. We didn't understand what had happened. We were stunned, confused.

It was all so complex. How was Genny to know whether the spirit was of divine consciousness, or merely someone who had left his plane but had not moved onto other planes? Perhaps mediumship for Genny was premature. Perhaps many years of discipline were necessary.

Genny was angry. "I know the truth. I know my thoughts changed. I became afraid." We both walked into the night air, holding each other until we were home. I apologized for assuming she was not ready. Genny said, "I became afraid tonight. Next time things will be different."

During the night Genny became sick. I was sure it would pass by morning. It did not. The next day she lay in bed. She couldn't hold down any food. She rolled from side to side as if delirious, as a high fever raged in her body all day and through the night.

By the following day, I was getting worried. All of her symptoms persisted, and she felt terrible. I went to Paz to ask if Genny could take any medicine. "Medicine will not help her," Paz insisted. "It is a test. A true medium must depend wholly on God. Tomorrow if she is not better, I will come to give her a spiritual injection."

That night as I sat through the long hours of darkness with Genny, I felt so helpless, so powerless. I realized for the first time how much I had always trusted doctors and their antibiotics. Just having a doctor present was always reassuring, even when he didn't give any medicine.

Genny and I meditated together. I practiced laying-on-of-hands. But the truth was that it was difficult to work with someone very close to me. I could not see everything as perfect when I identified with her pain. To see Genny as being whole was more of a mental exercise than something coming from my heart. I was empathizing with her discomfort, instead of her magnificent perfection. Could I rally my knowledge of the truth? It seemed as if both of us were being tested. Neither of us could do anything. We could only wait and admit our dependence upon something greater.

By daybreak, Genny's fever was as high as ever. A heavy rain had started during the night. Now all the streets were flooded. Paz would not be able to reach us. I looked out at the water running over the curbs and between houses and felt helpless in this foreign place with its foreign ideas. I had to do something to help Genny. Paz couldn't come to us. I had to go to her.

What normally would be less than a twenty-minute walk took me more than an hour. At least I was doing something. "I'll ask Paz if Genny can take some aspirin for her fever," I thought. "Even some tea would give her strength." This was the third day of Genny's illness.

More than an hour later I reached Paz's house. She was gone. She had found someone to take her to Genny. During the hour it took me to return to Genny, I was very aware that my acting out of fear had accomplished nothing. Paz was sitting next to Genny when I entered the room. I sat down next to her. I could tell that Genny felt better just having Paz there. Neither of us felt alone now.

"No aspirin, no tea," Paz insisted. "This is your test. Every medium must come to fully depend upon God. If a tea did help, you would not know if the tea were your healer, or God. Back home, your patients can take medicine. But you must know that God alone is more than enough to heal." Paz took her Bible and gave Genny a spiritual injection, pulling the energy from its pages.

Two more days passed and Genny's fever had not lessened. At this point, she hadn't eaten a meal in five days. The vomiting that followed each attempt to eat had left her stomach raw and painful. Paz came again and gave her more spiritual injections to improve her strength.

Genny was changing. Not only physically, but she also seemed different mentally. In the middle of her physical despair, I could see her letting go, releasing herself into something new. Her body was growing weaker, but in that weakness, she was giving way to a new strength deep within her. But there were moments when I doubted. Was Genny surrendering—or was she simply giving up? There is such a fine line between the two. When I looked at her physical being, I thought she might be giving up. But when I saw her spiritually, I was certain she was reaching a deep level of total surrender. I had my own test now. With which eyes would I see her?

The afternoon of the sixth day, Paz sent word that Sister Rose had communicated telepathically that she was coming to town for Genny's initiation. Sister Rose, Eduardo, and Paz were to be the three mediums performing Genny's ceremony of mediumship.

The message was delivered almost nonchalantly, as if Genny were perfectly well and of course looking forward to the visit and the ceremony. In fact, the way the message was given could have been seen as insensitive. But both Genny and I were heartened by Paz's lightheartedness. It strengthened both of us. Genny sat up in bed for the first time in six days. We held each other. She said, "I know now that I do not have to get out of the way for another being to speak through me. I must become that being. I am that being. There is no separation."

That evening she was out of bed, walking. Sister Rose arrived late. The big laugh coming from her frail little body caused both of us to rebound even more. "Tomorrow," she said, "we are going to initiate Genny and bless your flag. It will be a glorious day."

It was now Sunday, time for the initiation ceremony. Genny was still weak when she entered the church and walked down the aisle to stand before the congregation. Sister Rose, Paz, and Eduardo entered trance first. Standing between them, Genny, too, went into trance. A better way to describe it is to say that Genny went into knowing. As we watched, she was transformed. She became more radiantly beautiful than I had ever seen her. Her face lit up as the light of her being united with the light of a greater being.

The words she was speaking were only a small part of the awareness of peace she had brought into the church. There was a warm current of light and love flowing in the room, bathing each person there. We were all transported into a celestial place with her. Genny's initiation was a success. It was done. She was now a medium.

It was time to celebrate on this plane. We were eating barbecued duck and listening to Sister Rose's jokes before we knew it. It seemed that the entire village had come to Paz's house to offer congratulations and enjoy the party. In the festive commotion, I looked at Genny. She was different, yet she was the same. So was I. I was beginning to understand mediumship from a higher level. Genny said, "It was like watching myself in a dream. I was conscious of myself talking, yet I was watching myself talk." The importance of the trance was not in what was being said but in providing a channel to bring a heavenly presence into the reality of this world.

We were thankful for everyone's help, especially Sister Rose's. Coming down from the mountains through flooded roads, she had risked so much to take part in the ceremony. She would return to her home that same afternoon. I decided to go with her, just to be alone with her for awhile. Somehow I knew this would be our last time together.

On the long ride back into the mountains, there was one question that I wanted to ask her. Only her answer could give me what I sought. It was a long time before I could bring myself to ask the question. Finally, I turned to her, ready to ask. The expression on her face told me she already knew what I was about to say. "Sister Rose, what is my life's purpose?"

She grinned and opened her hands, taking one of mine. Then she said simply, "To know the power of prayer."

She said nothing more. The question was asked. The answer had been given. I continued to hold her hand as we watched the water pour off the jeep onto the road. She knew, as I knew, that the most difficult thing for me was to live fully while trusting the unknown. Prayer is the bridge between living my life and trusting whatever that life presents to me.

Late that evening I arrived back home. We had taken Sister Rose only halfway home. Someone else was there to take her the rest of the way.

The party was still in full swing. Genny had gone home to rest and had returned to meet me. Paz was just beginning her usual evening entertainment. She had invited everyone into her livingroom. She was going to go into trance again.

Paz said, "I travel to the records to get permission to look up any questions you have."

As we watched, Paz appeared to be literally ascending into heaven. Her eyes reflected a celestial light. She was waving to angels on the way. And when she met St. Peter at the gate and asked permission to enter, it was as if we were all there with her at heaven's gate. Paz was representing us, asking humbly to enter.

Finally she reached the records. It was explained to us that a medium has gold or silver files. If the name is erased, it means the person is going to die. If a name is blurry, this person is between life and death.

We had heard Doris speak of such files, or Akashic records, as they are called in other esoteric cultures. Paz was now obviously seated in a special building which contained the files. It was like a large marble library, where some people were moving about and others were looking up information in the files. Paz said, "Each of you is being granted three questions."

One woman asked, "How will my new store do?"

Someone else asked about a daughter who had died sometime ago. To this question, Paz answered that she would go and check. Moments later, Paz's voice changed. Suddenly a younger and much softer voice of a girl was speaking through her. Someone translated for us. We listened and watched the mother cry with tears of joy as we all heard the incredible description of heaven.

The woman's daughter was now speaking directly to other members of her family, who were also in the room. Her death was particularly tragic, because it had followed a long illness. She was apologizing for causing so much suffering, but she said that everything had happened in order for a greater plan to unfold. She was only eight at the time. Before dying she had said, "Mommy, I now go to heaven." She said that for a long while after she died, she had rested. But now she was in service with a group of angels who looked after young children. She was very happy. That night, for a few moments, everyone in the room felt that they had truly been in heaven with her.

Paz returned to the files and answered more questions. Paz's sister asked for a blessing. Smiles flickered through the group. Someone whispered, "This is a special time. Only this week her sister converted to Espiritism."

We remembered Paz's story. Seventeen years ago when she was sick and had the visions that led her to become a medium, the whole family had resisted. They had argued with her and even insulted her for believing. Yet Paz knew it was her test. She did not argue back. She would go to her room in tears and pray for hours. And tonight, after seventeen years, the last member of the family was finally willing to accept who she was.

To see Paz going to heaven and risking sharing the truth of a higher reality with this room full of people of varying degrees of faith gave us great joy. In honoring the truth of her gift, Paz embraced us and invited us to seek our highest self as well. "This is what a true spiritual teacher is," I thought. It would have been a crime if Paz had become a schoolteacher simply because that was what had been expected of her. Perhaps the greatest crime we all commit is not taking the risk to develop our own unique gifts. What the healers had taught us was the great variety of ways God has for expressing the truth through all of us.

I sat there trying to imagine living again at home in the West. How could I encourage people to find their own unique ways to experience and express their divine selves?

The questions continued. A man asked, "How will I support my family if I go back into the mountains on a mission to serve victims of the floods?"

Paz asked for a peso. She took it, blessed it, and wrapped it in a note of paper. "I could give you a thousand pesos," she said, "but they could be spent and you would someday be poor again. Or I can give you one peso and bless it, and know you will never be in need." Then she said, "You can never serve others unless you have served your family. You will take your place with your spiritual brothers as you heal and forgive the conflicts you have with your own family. Finding forgiveness at home may be far more difficult than going into the mountains to help victims of the floods. Finding forgiveness at home frees you from your karmic ties so you can truly be of God's service."

Then Paz turned to Genny and me. "You must teach that spiritual growth always begins at home. The heart most committed to God can lead nowhere until it has loved and found healing within its own family. Then one's heavenly family is found naturally with them."

At that moment it all seemed so simple. Everyone is given two sets of parents, one biological and one heavenly. When we become friends with our biological parents, when we understand and accept one another, we are released, or born again, into a greater family, our spiritual family. As we recognize our Mother and Father God, everyone becomes our brothers and sisters. Our disappointments are a part of being human. Our joy and our pain serve a greater purpose. Both are necessary parts of the climb to self-acceptance for each of us. This must be why all great spiritual teachers are so divinely human. They are not concerned about or ashamed of their weaknesses.

I looked at Genny and saw her glowing in the evening's setting. It was no accident that a part of her had to die before she opened to something greater. Our fear of death is our greatest obstacle to inner peace. As I watched Paz converse with the forces of heaven, I found myself thinking, "If the whole world could be here right now, climbing to heaven with Paz and listening to loved ones speak of their experience since leaving their bodies, we would all know the truth." We would not be so frightened of shedding our skin so we could grow closer to our spirit. Paz's beautiful face told it all.

It was obvious that the party would continue for hours, but Genny and I were too exhausted to stay. We slipped out quietly. The rainclouds overhead made the night sky even blacker. As we cautiously walked out onto the muddy street, a patch of bright moonlight suddenly lit our way. It guided us home.

The next morning we read from the *Course* before getting out of bed:

> *"The truly helpful are invulnerable because they are not protecting their egos, and so nothing can hurt them. The truly helpful are God's miracle workers, whom I direct until we are all united in the joy of the Kingdom. I will direct you to wherever you can be truly helpful, and to whomever can follow my guidance through you."*[71]

We lay in bed a long time that morning. Our stay in the Philippines was ending. We both knew our time here was complete. We ate lunch with Paz and spoke of this. She agreed our departure was imminent. She urged us to meditate more and pray that our gifts would be received. That afternoon, while in trance, she gave us spiritual flower petals to protect us from being led into temptation.

The day we went to say goodbye to Old Man Eduardo, he was limping. An ox in the field had knocked him down. He was upset because he was in too much discomfort to go into trance and bless our journey home. We laughed and loved him even more for being so open and vulnerable with us. He was a simple old man trying to give us his best advice as he said goodbye. He wanted to be certain we had one more gift before leaving. He took out his Bible and said, "Pray. Then open it three times and point. Each passage your finger is led to should have a similar message." I tried it. Two passages felt related, but I couldn't find the meaning in the third one. He laughed. "Genny, you try it." It was the same for her. Two passages were definitely related, but the third was unclear. Eduardo laughed again. "No, you have not failed. But you must practice."

We said goodbye to Eduardo, knowing that we would also not see him again, at least not on this side.

A few days later we left the Philippines and flew to San Francisco. As soon as we left the plane and walked into the airport, we felt the difference in cultures with the frantic movement in the terminal. Everyone was so busy, in such a hurry. Our plane had arrived early, so we sat on the curb while we waited for our good friend, Peter, to pick us up. We were like two flowers plucked out of the ground waiting to be replanted. As I watched people passing by, intensely on their way, I felt naked and alone. Then I noticed Genny smiling as she watched the same people. I looked again. This time I realized that I had been seeing a reflection of my old self, the empty shell I had endlessly tried to fill with new hopes and desires which would never be satisfied. In that moment, I saw very clearly just how powerful my thoughts could be. One fleeting thought, remembered by my old self, had the power to keep me from feeling that I was home. It had had the power to make me think that we are the flowers plucked out of the earth waiting for events to replant us, instead of knowing that we are always planted in God. And all the people we were watching were part of the same garden.

Genny pulled out our worn copy of the *Course*. She prayed, opened the book, and pointed, as Eduardo had done with the Bible:

* * *

"I am here to be truly helpful. I am here to represent Him who sent me. I do not have to worry about what to say or what to do, because He who sent me will direct me. I am content to be wherever He wishes, knowing He goes there with me. I will be healed as I let him teach me to heal."[72]

I took the book, held it, and reached within myself, asking to know. I opened it and pointed:

"I place the peace of God in your heart and in your hands, to hold and share. The heart is pure to hold it, and the hands are strong to give it."[73]

Genny took the book one more time, put it to her chest, and looked inside:

"Only the Holy Spirit knows what you need for He will give you all things that do not block the way to light. He gives you all the things that you need have and will renew them as long as you have need of them ... He knows that everything you need is temporary, and will but last until you step aside from all your needs and realize that all of them have been fulfilled."[74]

Epilogue

✦✦

In 1977, Bruce and Genny Davis returned from the Philippines. For ten years they directed a spiritual center in Marin County, California, serving many hundreds of people. At this time, they each discovered that their personal goals had changed, and so their lives went into new directions.

Today, Genny Wright Davis is an internationally-recognized Transformational Healer with a private practice in San Francisco, calling her work "Sacred Therapy." Her primary focus is to support the essence of a person's heart and soul beneath the defenses where inner healing emerges from one's own true nature.

Genny is director of the Center for Spiritual Healing of Marin County, Inc., California, as well as co-director of "The Path of the Adventurer," an intensive seminar for therapists and educators in Japan, Hawaii, and California. She also offers Shamanic and spiritual intensives throughout the country and in Europe.

For many years, she has traveled and studied with the Shamans of Peru, lived with the Espiritista healers of the Philippines, and apprenticed with an Alaskan Shaman.

Genny holds a degree in Psychology and Spiritual Healing, is a mother, and is co-author of four books, including *Hugs & Kisses.*

Genny can be contacted at the Center for Spiritual Healing, P.O. Box 1123, Fairfax, CA 94930.

Bruce Davis, Ph.D., since writing *The Heart of Healing*, has written *My Little Flowers*, and he is the author of *The Magical Child Within You.*

Bruce teaches at the School of Consciousness at John F. Kennedy University in Orinda, California and is founder of Spring Grove, Inc., in Marin County, California, where he offers weekly meditation groups, individual counseling, and healing. Bruce leads spiritual retreats in many parts of the United States and Europe. People from many countries have been touched by the simplicity, humility, and great love in these retreats. Each retreat supports people in their humanness while discovering their spiritual gifts and how to lead a richly spiritual, satisfying life.

Every year Bruce leads pilgrimages to Assisi, Italy, the home of St. Francis and St. Clare and other sacred places. Bruce is remarried, a father, and spiritual friend and teacher for many people.

For more information about Bruce's work, please write: Bruce Davis, Spring Grove, P.O. Box 807, Fairfax, CA 94930.

Reference

A Course In Miracles

1. T. 50
2. M. 9
3. T. 9
4. T. 518
5. T. 216
6. T. 82
7. W. 65
8. T. 563
9. W. 233
10. T. 490
11. W. 231
12. T. 57
13. T. 139
14. W. 85
15. W. 118
16. M. 55
17. W. 51
18. T. 203
19. T. 34
20. T. 261
21. T. 148
22. T. 75
23. T. 43
24. T. 167
25. W. 76
26. T. 523
27. T. 458
28. T. 12
29. T. 342
30. M. 58

38. T. 317
39. T. 76
40. T. 379
41. T. 146
42. T. 156
43. T. 414
44. T. 7
45. T. 100
46. T. 153
47. M. 25
48. T. 101
49. T. 10
50. T. 144
51. T. 511
52. T. 151
53. T. 107
54. W. 422
55. W. 247
56. T. 208
57. T. 227
58. T. 365
59. T. 374
60. W. 422
61. T. 247
62. W. 56
63. T. 73
64. W. 79
65. W. 64
66. T. 270
67. T. 215

31. T. 227	68. T. 105
32. T. 127	69. T. 292
33. T. 15	70. T. 108
34. T. 492	71. T. 65
35. W. 63	72. T. 24
36. W. 380	73. T. 76
37. T. 118	74. T. 239

T. Text   W. Workbook   M. Teacher's Manual

Foundation for Inner Peace
P.O. Box 635
Tiburon, California 94920